B. J.'s
PROMISE

HOW MY DYING DOG
FOUND MY TRUE LOVE

Jeaninne Escallier Kato

Dogs have a way of
finding the people
who need them.

Thom Jones
American writer, 1945 – 2016

ACKNOWLEDGMENTS

For Dr. Laura Pasten, DVM, for loving B.J. as her own,
and for sacrificing her personal life to save my girl.

Special thanks to everyone in this book who helped me become the person I am today. (Several names have been changed to protect the innocent.)

Many writers worked hard to make this book possible. Mila Johansen, author, book coach, and editor, believed in this story and my talent to tell it.

With great affection, I thank my writing group "Words Without Boundaries" (within Gold Country Writers) for their constant advice and support: Phillip Jacques, Del Whitely Dozier, Kate Luce, Brenda Sue Pignata, and Sarah Pressler.

To the talented and patient, Margaret Campbell, this is my huge hug for designing and producing this book.

Above all, none of this would be in print if the mysterious Asian man had not crossed my path on May 1st, 1994.

Thank you, Glenn Kato, my love, for accepting B.J.'s urgent plea to love me in her place.

B.J., you will always be that one dog who loved me enough to find my true love. "Mommy loves you."

There are no accidents in this life.

CONTENTS

CONTENTS

CHAPTER ONE

BEN

B.J., tied up behind a black iron stairwell on the side of a white stucco building, yelps in fear. I don't know how long she's been there—days, weeks, months. I'm not sure she's still alive. I don't remember losing her or how she escaped my care. In one scene, we run mountain switchbacks, sharing our passion for the great outdoors. In the next scene, I search desperately for her in a dark forest, bereft and alone. Before I can reach her to untie her emaciated body, I bolt upright from a deep sleep, the tears streaming down my face. That dream first appeared at the onset of my Golden Retriever's failing kidneys. When her voracious appetite disappeared, I knew it was the beginning of the end of our love story.

Twenty-five years have passed since her death. If I didn't know that one dog, destined to be mine, I wouldn't have the life I have today. B.J.'s story deserves to be told.

Ricky, sassy and sultry, arrived late to the crowded Santa Monica folk club that breezy summer night in June, 1983. In her usual style, she displayed the cleavage of her ample bosom, wearing clothes that accentuated her curvy body. I admired Ricky's shoulder-length, red curly hair and quick wit. By contrast, my runner's body—flat chested, with a long waist and strong limbs—represented the antithesis of a sexy bombshell. My chestnut brown, wavy hair fell to the middle of my back. I had that sparkly, girl-next-door enthusiasm. Ricky kept me calm and centered.

I yelled in her ear above the din of the bluegrass band.

"I can't believe I grabbed the last two seats at the bar. Ricky, see that guy sitting next to me, isn't he adorable? I don't think he's interested because I couldn't engage him in a conversation." Ricky winked at me as if to say, *I've got this.*

Ricky leaned across me, igniting a conversation with the tall, bearded man sporting thick, shaggy auburn hair. His dark blue eyes, shielded by arched sun-bleached eye brows, ignited a desire I hadn't felt in years. I imagined if he were to shave his beard, his straight nose, high cheekbones, and full lips would be the face of Old Spice cologne. I moved down one seat so Ricky could talk to him. I sensed he liked her savvy New Jersey confidence better than my apologetic California cool.

When this perfectly proportioned man rose to use the bathroom, Ricky whispered, "Jeaninne, he's shy. Try talking to him again." Ricky guided me back into the seat next to Ben. When he returned, he looked directly into my eyes and smiled. I felt the blood rush from my head to my toes.

"I'm Ben. Can we start over?" I shook his extended hand, yearning to prolong the warm strength of his grip. I hoped he felt the connection, as well.

Ben spoke easily about his life as a forest ranger in Alaska before this recent trip to visit his sister and her husband in Pasadena, California. He found this funky folk club from a bulletin board in a Pasadena coffee house. I enjoyed sharing my enthusiasm for teaching Learning Disabled teens in Santa Monica, as well as expressing my desire to find permanence in a different community I could afford. Ben asked me to meet him the following night in the same club to listen to a new band. He didn't mention Ricky.

After two nights of listening to L.A.'s best folk bands, while trying to talk over live music in a small space, Ben asked me on a legitimate date. We spent our third night together over sushi in a beachfront bistro where we didn't have to yell over blaring instruments and loud patrons. As he spoke, I fell into the spell of Ben's Irish blue eyes and classically sculpted face.

Ben, more relaxed to open up about his life in a quiet atmosphere, shared his life easily. "I had to leave Illinois as a teen. City life was slowly strangling me. When I moved to Colorado to live with my mother's cousins, I found my soul in God's country—the great outdoors. One of my high school teachers, a Jesuit priest, almost pleaded with my mother to do something to change my life; he feared my depression would devour me. That's when Mom knew I needed to leave Chicago. In essence, she saved my life." When he spoke of his mother, he glowed.

I ignored the part about his propensity for depression, feeling assured his mother had found the fix. I continued with my story.

"I found my soul in teaching, but I can't afford to keep living in a studio apartment on rent control. I feel blessed to have the Pacific Ocean in my back yard and everything I enjoy about Los Angeles in my front yard. On a teacher's salary, I couldn't own a home in this area. I'm thinking about relocating to Northern California where there is open land and a cheaper cost of living. I just can't be too far from my mother, my best friend."

Yet, my thoughts were saying otherwise, *Ben, tell me where to go and I'll follow you anywhere.*

We soon discovered that our thoughts matched that evening, *How can I fit this fabulous person into my life?* As we pushed into our thirties, settling down with our soulmate was at the top of our lists. I went to bed that night with only one thought. *Could he be the one?*

I knew immediately that Ben had issues with self-esteem and depression, but his good looks, kindness and intelligence swept all my reasoning out to sea. I attributed his extreme shyness to living a remote mountain lifestyle. As a park ranger in Alaska, Ben had lived alone for years in a mountain cabin, relying on his passion for the outdoors to get him through some bleak times of self-doubt and isolation.

Ben didn't try to hide his dark side from me. He seemed relieved to unburden some of his most forbidden thoughts.

"I was so lonely in Alaska, I had recurring thoughts of suicide. I used to fantasize about speeding through red lights, hoping someone would take me out. Then I realized I might harm others and came to my senses." I noticed his perfectly weathered face furrowed with pain. I fell right into my Florence Nightingale teaching mode. I was certain I could make Ben love himself.

I didn't blink. Being young, in love, and wanting everything the white picket fence implied, I naively assumed that loving a positive woman would cure Ben of the blues that had plagued him most of his life. I declared, "Well, you don't have to look back on that life. There isn't anything we can't accomplish together." I squeezed his hand; he squeezed back.

While enjoying the summer in my second-story apartment with a distant view of the Pacific Ocean, we began making plans for the future. Within a few weeks, Ben's gregarious Irish American parents flew out from Chicago to meet me and my large multicultural family. Mom had already planned a pool party in the modest Orange County home she shared with my stepfather. The party, originally arranged for celebrating my recent Masters Degree in Education, landed at the perfect time to join our families.

Our families gelled around the succulent smells of barbecue meat, the happy laughter of children splashing in the pool, and my family and friends genuine support. Our love exploded so fast, I chose not to heed the storm clouds that began to accumulate in the horizon of our knowing.

After two idyllic summer months together, I resigned from my teaching position without regrets. Ben decided to leave Palmer, Alaska, for good. By late August, he drove his bronze Volkswagen truck, pulling a U-Haul trailer of mostly my belongings, while I drove my royal blue Honda Civic, carrying boxes, clothes, and my Siamese cat, Boogers, to Park City, Utah. I didn't want to take the mountains out of the man, nor did Ben want to take the woman too far from her family.

We compromised on a location we thought would be a solid fit for both of us—a ranger job for Ben, a teaching position for me. My childhood friend, Gail, urged me to apply for an available teaching position at the new elementary school outside of town. We stayed in her Park City home until we found a place. Destiny had arrived sooner than expected.

CHAPTER TWO

PARK CITY

I secured the only available teaching position as a K-4 Resource Specialist at Parley's Park Elementary a week before the opening of school. Ben couldn't find a ranger position, so he accepted a construction job, which contributed to the vastly growing ski resort town of Park City. Within two months of our initial meeting, we journeyed from our previous lives and found a new state to start our lives together. I grappled with my choice—genius or insanity? Either way, love grabbed the wheel and we let go.

We rented a two-bedroom basement apartment of an A-frame home in the sprawling ranch lands a few miles from town. From the large kitchen/living room picture window, we saw herds of cattle grazing in the foreground flanked by the slopes of Park West Ski Resort (now The Canyons) against the Wasatch Mountain Range. The juxtaposition of verdant flat land against rugged gray mountains sent me back into another time. We had the best of nature within our reach.

Afraid our Mormon ranching neighbors would protest and want to remove me as their children's teacher for not being married to the man with whom I lived, we planned our wedding for the following spring in Southern California. We wanted to give Ben's family in Illinois enough time to arrange their attendance. We set the date for April 15, 1984.

Our Mormon neighbors couldn't have been more lovely about our living situation. They often showed up with baked goods and tools we desperately needed. Ben volunteered his services with cabinetry and car maintenance. One family thanked me for being such a caring teacher. We existed in a fog of happiness. Until the clouds cleared.

I threw myself into my work. Coming from a self-contained seventh, eighth, and ninth- grade Special Education classroom full of mostly unruly boys at John Adams Middle School in Santa Monica, I revamped how I approached the sweet kindergarten through fourth-grade students in a pull-out Resource classroom at Parley's Park. Late evenings and both weekend days were devoted to researching the Utah standards, as well as setting up a hands-on, fun classroom stocked with Apple computers and art projects.

I swelled with excitement and anticipation when I entered my colorful classroom full of curious children. They waited each morning to be dazzled by their quirky teacher who didn't look like the other Mormon teachers. I tried to fit in with button-down, long-sleeve shirts and calf-length, wool skirts, but I felt like I was wearing variations of a straight jacket, my arms tied down to my sides. I couldn't move freely in those clothes. Once I returned to wearing flouncy skirts and embroidered peasant blouses, I could breathe again.

The staff at Parley's taught me how to raise my standards. I had to maintain their high educational standards, so I worked twice as hard as the contract required. They learned to accept my free-spirited ways and I respected their professional ethics. Parley's Park Elementary School gave me a strong foundation on which to build upon. I wanted to be a multifaceted educator with the discipline to match as demonstrated by my esteemed colleagues.

My classroom windows faced the imposing Wasatch Mountains. I couldn't contain the joy I felt witnessing the explosion of fall in iridescent colors of orange, yellow, and red when I began my 1983-84 teaching year—I wanted this marriage to work more than anything. As the year progressed, the mountains transformed into a winter wonderland of crystalline white. By spring, they were covered in glorious hues of green and gold. I was falling hard for the clear, crisp Park City air, 8,000 feet above sea level. My mountain man added the security I needed to risk living in extreme conditions.

Ben and I were like children discovering the mountains for the first time; we couldn't get enough of them. We skied the downhill resorts at night on groomed runs illuminated by giant floodlights. The snow turned into rainbow-colored crystals before our eyes.

On the weekends, we preferred cross-country skiing in the hills behind our home, followed by two-night camping trips high above the mountain resorts. Those full moon nights bathed the fields of snow in sparkling lunar light. I never grew weary of the silent mystery of winter. Yet, the starlight of our union had begun to dim.

Ben loved me, but his insecurities began creeping into our relationship like weeds growing up through The Yellow Brick Road. The ways I showed my enthusiasm for our love didn't seem to connect with his sensibilities; and, at times, he saw my exuberance as something negative.

Summer turned to fall. The Trix-colored mountains added to my feeling of exhilaration. We changed our lives in the span of two months. The dramatic transformation of seasons reminded me of the love that hypnotized us to move so quickly.

"Finally, a date night," I exhaled as we merged onto Parley's Canyon Road, the main mountain highway connecting Park City to Salt Lake City. "We've been so busy setting up our lives, we haven't taken time to enjoy an evening out together." I dressed in my fancy jeans, black turtleneck, leather jacket and suede boots. I even curled my hair. My cheeks hurt from smiling. Ben looked ravishing in his beige suede jacket, cobalt blue plaid shirt and tight Levi's. I made a mental note to buy him cowboy boots for his upcoming 31st birthday.

"Ben, when is the last time we've been down to Salt Lake together?"

No response. Ben gripped the steering wheel and stared straight ahead.

"Are you okay?" I snuggled into his neck.

He answered me with a furrowed side glance.

"Did I say something wrong?" I sat up straight.

Ben accelerated down the canyon a bit too fast for my comfort. I felt anger and fear fighting for dominance in my solar plexus.

After a long pause, he spoke, "Why do you have to be so cheerful all the time?"

Like being kicked in the stomach, I couldn't speak for a few minutes. Once my breathing regained its normal rhythm, I mustered up an answer.

"What can I say to that question? I'm happy to be going on an official date with my fiance. How else do you expect me to act? I'm so confused right now."

Ben had nothing to say. His face remained emotionless as he stared into the horizon.

The night was ruined. We endured the rest of the evening in a palpable silence, pretending to enjoy a boisterous dinner atmosphere at Benihana's, occasionally swapping a few words about work, while the Asian chefs chopped meat, flipped fish, and entertained the enthusiastic diners at our extended table. We watched the movie "The Right Stuff" without touching or holding hands. Petrified, I felt my idyllic mountain life with my ideal man had begun to crack and I wouldn't know how to put back the pieces.

We drove home under a blanket of sadness.

"Ben, I'm sorry I upset you, but you know whatever you think I did was not anything conscious on my part." My breathing became shallow.

Ben reached for my hand and said, "I know. I don't know why I react so extremely to insignificant behaviors. I'm sorry I made you feel so sad. You didn't do anything."

Then why did I feel punished?

Too exhausted to talk when we walked in the door, we fell into bed. By morning, I wanted to forget the night before ever happened. We never mentioned it, again.

Late that October, I joined an aerobics instructor training class in Salt Lake City because the sports lodge in Park City expressed interest in hiring me. As I left the class at dusk to drive the thirty-nine miles back up the mountain to Park City, the air cut my skin like sharp ice. Being born and raised in Southern California, I never thought about the hazards of driving in inclement weather, other than heavy rain every now and then. With high-altitude living, I had no idea how quickly conditions change at the slightest drop in temperature.

Ben's Volkswagen truck rode low to the ground. With the restricted acceleration a diesel vehicle can muster in normal driving conditions, the truck struggled up Parley's Canyon. My instincts told me that I was in for a ride that would test the boundaries of my driving ability, not expecting to stretch the limits of my worst fear.

In the mid-1980's, Parley's Canyon was a dark, steadily climbing road that connected Salt Lake City to the mountain resort town of Park City. Only seasoned truckers and local mountain people drove it at night. Within the 39-mile stretch, the elevation rose from sea level to 7,149 feet along the western Wasatch Range.

On one side, a sheer wall rose like a monolith; on the other side, nothing. If you veered off the road, you rolled down a steep embankment. Today, the roads are wider with permanent guard rails.

White flecks of powdered snow assaulted my windshield. Like the view of a child's kaleidoscope, swirling psychedelic patterns of snowflakes obliterated my view. I looked to the left. Darkness. I looked to the right. Darkness. I forgot to breathe.

My primitive brain kicked in and switched onto one thought that flapped around and around in my mind like a broken 16mm movie reel, *If you stop, you will be buried alive in snow drifts.* I drove five miles per hour, hugging a mountain wall I couldn't see.

I couldn't feel my body. I had shifted into survival mode.

When I looked into my rear-view mirror, I saw him. The driver of a semi-truck, his headlights flashing into my rear window, signaled for me to follow. As he pulled out to maneuver his rig in front of me, my body let go and I sobbed uncontrollably. God had sent me a lifeline in the form of a truck-driving angel.

I followed him to the Kimball Junction Exit. I had been gripping the steering wheel so tightly, it hurt to open my fingers. Once we hit the lit intersection, I prayed the driver would stop so I could thank him in person. Instead, he honked, waved, and disappeared into the driving snow.

I entered the house a sniffling mess of hot tears. With clear snot running down my face, I fell into Ben's arms. He responded with detached indignation as I retold the events of my harrowing drive.

"I don't understand why you're so emotional, it's only the first light snow of the season." Ben held me outstretched from his body as if he were chastising a small child.

I felt blindsided all over again. "Light snow! I couldn't see the road at all through white-out conditions. You know how dark that canyon is at night. I could have driven over the edge!" My face resembled a toddler who isn't being understood by the adults around her—contorted, red, pleading, holding back frustrating screams. I couldn't believe his callous lack of concern for my safety!

"Well, if you're going to be a mountain woman, you better toughen up." Ben let go of my shoulders, turned on his heels, and escaped into the bedroom. I *was* that toddler being misunderstood and ignored. I felt abandoned, angry, helpless, and sad. I didn't know where to put any of those feelings, so I took refuge in the guest room, sobbing into my pillow until sleep took over.

Our relationship needed help.

CHAPTER THREE

B. J.

In late October, one of my colleagues mentioned that a prominent Park City family was selling purebred Golden Retriever puppies. My ears perked up. Ben and I once discussed being dog owners. I felt the time was ripe for a positive change in our relationship. I wrote down the information to share with him later that evening.

"Ben, remember soon after we met the fun we had camping in Big Bear with your sister's Labrador Retriever?" I practically panted at the thought of being a dog parent.

"Yeah, we had a great time with that big guy." A slight grin crossed Ben's face.

"Do you think the time is right for being dog parents? I have a lead on some Golden Retriever puppies from someone at work." I crossed my fingers behind my back.

"We could check them out." I held my breath in case Ben changed his mind.

Trying to quell my enthusiasm I said, "Right? I was thinking the same thing."

I couldn't sleep that night thinking about the possibility of our home filled with puppy love. I remembered a moment that I had tucked away in my memory years before.

When I attended California State University Fullerton, juggling two jobs, I often drove to Laguna Beach to clear my mind. I loved the bohemian dress shops and craggy shoreline that satisfied my restless soul. Laguna's picturesque coves catered to my creative yearnings. It was my place to breathe. Laguna holds the bulk of my best, bucolic beach days being an adolescent.

One summer day in 1975, while driving the two-lane highway through Laguna Canyon in my taupe '64 Volkswagen, I came to a four-way stop. To my left, sitting in the open cab of an old red truck, were two of the most beautiful dogs I had ever seen—the sun's light left a refracted halo around their golden coats. They grinned wide goofy smiles that reminded me of a scene in a New England travel brochure. I was smitten. I yelled out the window, "I will love a dog like you two beauties someday!" The driver honked and waved.

It's odd how that fleeting moment burned such a lasting memory. Maybe, it was a sign of what had already been written in the script of my life.

Ben picked me up after school to take a look at the puppies. I had been fantasizing about those puppies all day at work. I desperately hoped that a special dog, our dog, might be the glue to repair the cracks beginning to grow in our relationship. We needed a new focus.

The two-story house was located in one of the newer, up-scale neighborhoods of Park City. Children's toys and bikes filled the yard. I appreciated the contrast of resort wealth with childlike innocence. We were greeted by a dark-haired, attractive woman in her thirties who ushered us into the garage. The red silky mother dog laid comfortably on her bed with one pup, then three months old, romping playfully around her.

Mrs. Jansen explained that this last female puppy might not be available; they hadn't decided whether to keep her or sell her.

I didn't hear a word. I cradled that Buddha-belied baby in my arms.

"Jeaninne, did you hear what Mrs. Jansen said?" Ben tried to delicately extract the fluffy pup from my arms, knowing that once I set my mind to something there's no going back. I held on to her as if she were already ours.

I pleaded, "Mrs. Jansen, if there's any way you can understand that we were meant to have her, I can assure you that this puppy will be loved and cherished to her dying day."

Ben shrugged his shoulders. "I can't fight city hall."

Mrs. Jansen promised she would discuss it with her family. Since they already had both parent dogs, the children might agree. I hugged her tightly and thanked her profusely.

I waited exactly four days to hear from Mrs. Jansen again. I felt like a prisoner on death row waiting for the governor's pardon. Each agonizing day was torturous. That golden girl had to be ours.

"Hello, Jeaninne. My family agreed to let her go. You can pick her up anytime."

I screamed, "Ben, get in the car! She's ours!" I grabbed our coats and tossed the car keys at Ben's waiting hands.

We flew through the pet store to get all her needed supplies —food, toys, bed, bowls, leash, and collar. We even stopped by the local vet's office and made an appointment for an updated check-up. I wanted the Jansen family to rest assured that we were the best fit for this puppy.

The youngest son was playing with our dog in the yard when we drove up to the house. He said, "Every day this puppy follows me to the bus to bite the food from the bottom of my lunch bag. She got my apple one time before I could catch her."

I bent down and took his hands in mine. "Don't you worry, young man. Ben and I will love her as much as you have. Thank you so much for trusting us to be her forever home." He looked sad, which broke my heart.

After we squared away the details, I scooped our baby into my arms and never looked back. I couldn't bear seeing that child's goodbye.

"Ben, what are we going to name her?" I wanted her named before we entered the long gravel driveway that led to our basement apartment.

"I don't know," Ben answered. "Maybe we need to sleep on it."

"How about the initials B.J. for Ben and Jeaninne?"

"I like it. Strong, yet personal." Ben smiled for the first time in days.

I snuggled our golden girl into my chest and said, "B.J. it is." Ben roughed up the feathers on B.J.'s fluffy head.

The puppy energy in our home swept out the looming darkness of doubt in our marriage. Our jobs took on new meaning—we had another being to raise. The aerobics routines I taught at the sports club to Michael Jackson's "Thriller" album were fueled by the creative juices inspired by this amazing dog. Ben and I had a purpose.

Ben softened to my emotional ways and I forgot about second-guessing the marriage. Even my cat, Boogers, found this curious canine a fascinating creature. She watched B.J. from the safety of her high places around the house, hissing to let this precocious puppy know who was really in charge. Soon enough, they became true friends, often cuddled together in front of the fireplace. B.J. gave all of us a refreshing lease on life.

We brought her home in late November. Ben built B.J. a dog house as a warm refuge for her playtime in the snow. She so enjoyed being outside during the day, she never once entered that dog house. Her rightful shelter was in the house with us, so B.J. made the most of her outdoor time: rolling, running, chewing, and fetching.

I couldn't wait to get home each day to play with our rapidly growing girl. B.J. romped over the snow drifts like a gazelle over high grass. Ben and I rolled over and over in the deep snow with B.J. down the steep driveway, entangled together. Wedged between us like a hot dog between two buns, our laughter rang through the hills.

"Uh oh, Ben, someone had an accident." We weren't paying enough attention to her whimpers on an especially cold Saturday afternoon. We thought she was merely anxious to be outside. We both felt guilty for missing this urgent request, her independent attempt at potty training. It wasn't her fault.

Ben pointed to the puddle in the rug and apologized, "Good girl, B.J. We are so sorry we didn't realize you were trying to do the right thing." Then, he scooped B.J. into his arms and carried her outside. Ben patiently waited while B.J. did her business.

He didn't know I watched through the window when he gathered her into his lap and let her slather him in kisses. Her love worked wonders on both of us.

No more accidents occurred in the house. B.J.'s intelligence matched her beauty—a sunlight-blonde fuzzy bear with chocolate brown eyes.

Our girl grew fast. Her paws sprouted to the size of small oven mitts. Her legs lengthened overnight to support those formidable feet. Soon, our baby's Buddha belly smoothed into a strong, muscular body, eventually reaching her optimal weight of eighty pounds. I often rested in the cove of B.J.'s warm belly, feeling the comfort of her silky, wavy coat, turning from corn-silk blonde to the shade of a sunset on fire.

Unlike the blonde retrievers bred in America, B.J. had the copper red coloring, broader head, and nose of the British bloodlines. She was an adorable puppy, but she transformed into a jaw-dropping show beauty. I couldn't imagine loving any dog more than I loved B.J.

I grew up in the suburbs of Southern California being allowed to have an aquarium, rodents, and cats. We acquired Missy, an auburn standard-size Dachshund, when I was five. She was my best friend until we had to put her down when I was nineteen.

I didn't have time to care for another pet until a month before I met Ben. I adopted Boogers from a family who could no longer care for her. Once I love a pet, nothing can tear me away from his or her care, no matter what changes occurred in my life.

B.J. knew everyone in the several-mile radius of our Park City ranch land. We included her in our daily run from the top of our hill to the main road. We made a complete five-mile circle, looping around the elementary school and Park West Ski Resort. B.J. lived for those runs. We didn't need to leash her because she instinctively knew to stay between us.

However, B.J., still a puppy, was too curious for her own good. On one of our daily runs around the ranch lands, we realized we had to enroll her in obedience school.

"Ben, look, Moose got out again." B.J. ran up to greet him. They both stood sniffing noses and wagging tails.

One evening after work, we had begun to run down our ridge road, leading out to the main road, when our neighbor's massive Golden Retriever, Moose, charged out to greet us. We patted Moose's white blonde, lion-size head, expecting him to saunter back into his yard, but he had other intentions.

Ben added to the myth of Moose. "Jeaninne, did you know that Moose once launched his body through the living room window to escape the house? I guess his family has tried everything to keep him corralled to the confines of his yard when they aren't home. Looks like nothing is working. Ranchers are known to shoot dogs that chase their livestock, which is legal in Utah. This goofy guy has had many close calls with a shot gun." I cringed at the thought.

After their friendly greeting, Moose hopped around B.J. like Michael Jordan ducking and dodging in and out of his opponents before slam-dunking a basketball. Moose dared B.J. to guard him so he could run up and down our neighborhood court. Before we could grab her, both of them tore out between the houses into the fields below. Hundreds of cows grazed contentedly.

Ben ran after B.J. with lightning speed. I stood slack-jawed, witnessing a potential stampede. The cows began running because Moose and B.J. nipped at their heels.

Ben yelled, "B.J.! Come!" The muscles in Ben's neck and face tightened until I thought they would snap.

B.J. stopped and looked back. For a second, she turned to follow Moose, but quickly realized her alpha dog meant business. Ben ran to B.J. and hauled her back up the hill by the scruff of her neck.

I know he was terrified she could have met the other end of a rifle. Our naive girl needed that wake-up call.

Moose obediently followed. When Ben and B.J. returned to me, Ben admonished Moose, "Go home big boy! You've caused enough trouble." Moose gave us a silly grin before he ambled back down the road from where he came.

We continued to run the same route; but, after that day, B.J. had to adapt to a leash. Moose was no longer allowed to join us.

The neighborhood children often knocked on our door asking if B.J. could play in our front yard. I enjoyed watching her catch wayward Frisbees and flying tennis balls. Her reward was an endless supply of hugs. However, after the cattle escapade with Moose, we enrolled B.J. in a local obedience class.

Roughly twenty canines from a cornucopia of dog breeds assembled in the town hall auditorium. B.J. stood fascinated. We witnessed a new side to our rambunctious puppy. She leaned into our legs and observed. We watched other owners pulling on their leashes to get their pups to obey. Not B.J. She seemed to know she was there to learn. Once the class began, B.J. didn't miss a command. Other dogs tried to distract her with barks and friendly sniffs, but our girl sat motionless, listening.

At the end of the four-week class, the instructor directed us to line up our dogs across the back of the auditorium. She told us to drop the leashes in front of our pups. With each raise of her arm, we stepped back one giant pace. We gave the arm out front with a flat hand command instead of the verbal "stay" command. Several dogs tumbled out of line like a house of cards. Ben and I couldn't control our laughter. We knew exactly how this was going to end.

B.J. remained sitting as still as a statue, looking straight ahead. Her eyes remained fixed on our faces. She waited for the next signal. By the time the participants, and all of their dogs, had returned to the instructor, B.J. was the only dog frozen in stay position on the other side of the room. For the first time, I knew what it felt like to be a proud parent.

My colleagues begged me to bring B.J. to school knowing how much the children would appreciate her beauty and calm demeanor. Ben often brought her to my classroom on Fridays for free-time rewards. For the children who finished their weekly work with passing grades, Ben supervised them on the playground to play fetch with B.J. while I worked with small groups in the classroom.

When Ben returned her to the classroom, B.J. cuddled with the children in the yellow bean bag chairs while they read to her. In those early days, I realized her innate power as an educator. B.J.'s work in the classroom had just begun.

We included B.J. in every aspect of our lives. She especially liked our bitter cold winter camping trips, eventually becoming the warmer, lighter spring and summer camping. Our fourteen-hour car trips between Utah and California were cake walks to B.J's peripatetic soul.

Ben's parents fell in love with her whenever they came for week-long visits. His father insisted she sleep with him on the air mattress by the fireplace. Ben's parents fought over who would walk her on our many hikes and trips into town. I am eternally grateful for all the photos showing B.J.'s loyalty to many friends, family, and students throughout our years together.

CHAPTER FOUR

NEVADA CITY

We planned a simple and festive wedding, though it was almost 100 degrees Fahrenheit on that Southern California spring day. On April 15th, 1984, we married in the Brea Methodist Church (we allowed our Catholic memberships to lapse years before). My mother made my Gibson Girl white cotton dress with three-quarter sleeves and a smocked bodice. I wore a large sun hat on top of a simple topknot, with wisps of loose hair flowing down my neck. A powder blue satin sash around my waist matched Ben's white tuxedo and powder blue cumberbund. Ben serenaded me on the guitar with a song he wrote especially for me.

We recruited friends and family to do the flowers and photos. The air-conditioned reception, held in the Spanish-style Brea Civic Center, revived the over-heated guests. We offered a chicken buffet dinner accompanied by the jazzy blues of my brother's rock band. Our large families blended well, making the day especially fun and stress-free. B.J. stayed with friends in Park City, but we wanted to get back to her as soon as possible. We spent only a few days on our honeymoon, seeing the typical tourist sights in San Diego. Our joy remained at home in Park City with our girl.

An important decision hung over us when my teaching year ended in June, 1984. Do we stay in a ski resort town with little or no forest ranger options for Ben? Or, do we move back to California where we could have a new start in our chosen fields, and I could be closer to my family? It made sense to move back to California.

I hate goodbyes. I chose to leave an ideal teaching position and wonderful new friends for Ben's happiness. I stuffed my feelings into a walled-off compartment of my heart to get through the goodbye party at work. The well-wishes from new friends and neighbors felt more like condolences. I wouldn't see most of those people again. The weekend school closed for the summer, we worked hard to walk out of our sparkling clean A-frame rental. I couldn't bear to prolong any more farewells.

B.J. and Boogers shook when they saw us packing up our belongings. I knew B.J. would miss the vast acreage in these ranch lands, but she would miss the neighborhood children even more. As if in protest, Boogers hid in her private nooks around the house. If we didn't have so much work to do, I would have disappeared into my own nook. This Southern California girl had fallen hard for the majestic mountains of Utah. These mountains led us to B.J., the love of our lives.

Moving day blurred as if it were fast-forwarded on record, speeding through unwanted commercials. We sprinted through cleaning and carrying boxes out of the house at a dizzying pace. When it was time to find Boogers, the tape froze. We had the cars and U-Haul trailer packed to the gills. Our basement apartment smelled of bleach. The new renters waited in the driveway. I felt beyond stressed.

"Ben, I can't find Boogers! I have scoured every corner of this place. She's gone." I paced back and forth between the car and the house.

"Jeaninne, we have to go. The new renters are losing patience." Ben wore his familiar scowl when exasperated with me.

I announced, "I WILL NOT LEAVE WITHOUT MY CAT!" I enlisted help from the new renters because Boogers was the other half of my heart.

I don't know what made me do it, but I suddenly thought to look under the front seat of Ben's truck. There, she hid. Her eyes beamed brightly and her body trembled in fear. I scooped Boogers out and held her close.

I cooed, "It's going to be okay, Bookish Mishtookus, we're going to start a new life. Look at B.J., she's excited to go." There sat our goofy girl, a long pink tongue, marked with one dark freckle, hanging out of her broad head.

B.J. reminded me of some ditzy society matron waiting to be chauffeured to some charity event. "Okay, B.J., we can leave now." I wanted to put a purple hat with netting on her head to complete my mental picture. I felt slap-happy with joy to have the whole family packed in and ready to go.

Ben apologized to the new renters and herded us into position—me, in my Honda with Boogers; Ben, in his Volkswagen truck with B.J. A new beginning. Again.

We decided to scout the Nevada City/Grass Valley area in the Sierra Foothills of Northern California. A fellow teacher told me about the beauty of the Gold Country and how it might be promising for a teacher and a forest ranger. We rolled the dice, hoping our credentials and experience would land us on our feet, wherever we planted our homestead flag.

Looking back, I understand how caution is wasted on youth. We were too naive to understand that life doesn't fall into an existence we imagined in our heads. I couldn't foresee that the next few years would be the hardest adult years of my life.

We spent our first night in a Nevada City motel where we walked B.J. along a stream bed while Boogers enjoyed the air-conditioned room. This foothill town, situated between the fingers of the Sierras, seemed to contain everything we had grown to appreciate. We had become accustomed to the mountain life in a small-town community. And hopefully, we would find satisfying jobs to keep us rooted there for a long time.

That same week, we managed to clear our first hurdle with ease by renting a cozy wood-framed bungalow situated behind a stately Victorian house. At 600 square feet, it had a bright living room, a long galley kitchen, a tiny bedroom, and a pass-through bathroom.

The bungalow sat in the center of two large yards. It was protected in a small valley alcove not far from town. Our few possessions fit perfectly in that 100-year-old cabin with yellowed flowered wallpaper and brown marbled carpets. Not our dream home, but good enough.

B.J. and Boogers adapted quickly to the tree-lined backyard filled with old Maples. The spacious, grassy front yard rimmed in giant redwoods on the right side of the house, lay adjacent to an overgrown lot that separated us from the neighbors up the hill.

The long driveway to the left of the porch butted against an iron fence redolent in blackberry bushes. Those bushes gave us privacy from our immediate neighbors and provided delicious berry cobblers on hot summer nights. B.J. and Boogers often grazed along those bushes, savoring those ripe berries like forbidden candy.

B.J. wasted no time meeting the neighbors.

One afternoon, as I sunbathed in the front yard, B.J. trotted up to me with a tiny girl trailing behind her.

"Oh, hello," I said. Upon closer inspection, I realized that the tiny girl was not a girl at all, but a young woman. I could see that this young woman had grave health issues. Her skin glowed a translucent purple. She couldn't have weighed over seventy pounds.

In a distorted voice that sounded like she had just inhaled helium, the frail girl said, "I adore your dog. She walked up to me, then pushed my hand with her nose like she wanted me to follow. I think she wants us to meet. My name is Aleasha. I live across the street."

"That's our girl, B.J. Everyone she greets is a friend. Nice to meet you, Aleasha." My heart melted.

I learned that this little elfin girl of seventeen was waiting for a heart/lung transplant. Her prospects for survival were bleak if she didn't get a heart soon. I imagined that B.J. smelled her illness and wanted to help. I held back my tears.

Aleasha felt extremely honored to have been chosen as the 7-11 National Cycling Association team mascot. All she could talk about was bike racing and being a celebrity. I couldn't contain my excitement for her. Every year, the NCA hosted bicycle races through Nevada City to promote the upcoming Tour de France. Thanks to B.J., Aleasha and her civic-minded family were our first contacts in Nevada City.

Tragically, Aleasha didn't make it to her twenty-fourth birthday. Her fragile body rejected the transplant, not bearing up under the complications. We had already moved away before we learned of Aleasha's death.

I reached out to the family, remembering how she was one of God's special ambassadors. B.J. knew Aleasha was an angel. B.J. visited her frail friend whenever she could sneak across the street without getting caught.

CHAPTER FIVE

JOBS

B en and I enjoyed the social aspects of living in an artsy town. I vowed to join a local theater group and expressed interest in becoming a disc jockey for the community radio station, KVMR. Ben wanted to do some volunteer work with at-risk teens. Until we found our first jobs, we hung out in our favorite cafes, attended music and theater events, and ran with B.J. out to the many lakes that dotted the periphery of our gold-mining town. We even managed to fit in several camping trips before the weather changed. My life in Park City dissipated into a distant memory.

By August, 1984, available teaching jobs in the Nevada City/Grass Valley did not exist. I mistakenly accepted the first job offered to me in the suburbs of Sacramento—a private school for severely emotionally disturbed teens. Ben found construction work in Sacramento, which made it convenient for us to carpool. Our money had sifted down to the bottom of the barrel. I needed to sign a teaching contract before the school year started.

We learned that B.J. stayed in the periphery of such a close-knit neighborhood. Boogers patrolled the lay of the land from our bedroom window. Ben nailed it partially closed with just enough space for her to enter and exit the house. The neighbors kept an eye on them.

B.J. assumed ownership of the whole block. She made her daily rounds from house to house, picking up odds and ends for her private stash. Our hidden road discouraged fast drivers; it was not a main artery into town. We knew every person who drove in and out of our forested enclave.

Within a few months of my teaching position as a math, English, and drama teacher with Schizophrenic teens, I knew something, other than dealing with severe mental illness, wasn't right with the administration.

Fortunately, I had two male aides who stepped in between me and an angry student who threw a chair or a table. The staff learned how to navigate around unstable behaviors fairly

quickly and efficiently. We relied on each other for support
not needed in public schools, much like soldiers in battle.
Unfortunately, something rotten lurked among the adults who
ran the school and housing units. Ten months into my teaching
year, the rumors of foul play broke open as shocking truths.

Ben picked me up at the school each day around 4 p.m.
for our drive into the foothills. Exhausted, discouraged, and
discontent with my job, I yearned for my positive and joyful
teaching position in Park City. However, once we drove down
the short hill into our valley hamlet, we witnessed our girl
happily chewing away on a treasure she had lifted from some
garage on the block.

When B.J. heard Ben's diesel engine, she sprang up
from her pile of "borrowed possessions" and ran to the car. I
couldn't get out fast enough to roll around on the grass with
her. Coming home to B.J. made our work lives almost bearable.

We arrived home one evening to two notes left on our front
porch. One was written in an adult's even hand; the other,
written in the scrawl of a preteen. I read the adult's note first.

Dear Neighbors,

For weeks, I have watched our wood pile slowly
shrink. It wasn't until I saw your dog pulling a log

from the side of the pile that I discovered the cause. When I tried to retrieve it, she ducked under your house. I'm sure you have much of our wood stashed under there. Please do something about your dog coming into our yard.

Thank you.

"Well, Ben, let's hope the next one isn't as daunting."

Dear Ben and Jeaninne,

You know how much I love B.J. She's part of our family. But it took me a month of odd jobs to earn enough money to buy my Nerf football. I looked in your yard full of B.J.'s toys where I found it all chewed up. Do you think you could replace it?

Your friend,

Kevin

We laughed knowing how hard it must have been for Aleasha's 13-year-old brother to write and rewrite this methodically crafted note. When we drove into the driveway, we even commented on the pieces of orange, spongy material spread over the lawn like confetti.

After we ran down to the game store in town to replace Kevin's Nerf ball, Ben checked under the house. Sure enough, a pile of uniformly chopped logs sat neatly stacked. We were impressed. Ben returned them the next day to the front Victorian house with the promise that we would fence in our backyard and keep the "thief" safely behind bars.

Ben spent that weekend fencing in our backyard. We also returned every single thing B.J. had lifted from neighboring garages. If we were going to remain in the good graces of our neighbors, we had to make some changes. B.J. wasn't happy.

She spent a week pouting under the back porch in the cool dirt. Not even a new Nerf ball of her very own, or her favorite big sticks from the lot behind us, changed the fact that B.J. had to conform to the iron-clad rules of being a town dog. B.J. missed visiting her friends most of all.

⌒

That first year in Nevada City did not bode well for our careers. Neither of us seemed to come up for air because of our long work days. We hated being away from B.J. Ben continued to look for forestry work to no avail and I was reaching my boiling point at work. He learned that forestry work was drying up in the foothills for white men over the age of thirty, due to women and minority quotas. Ben felt useless, obsolete.

My patience expired. "Excuse me, Assistant Director, may I have a word?" The female second-in-command was someone who walked softly carrying a big stick of arrogance, which I suspected was her shield against unwanted inquiries. The director and assistant director were an impenetrable force. However, after ten months of unanswered questions and dodgy behaviors around the school, I needed answers.

"Yes, Jeaninne, how may I help you?" The dragon lady stiffened.

"I ordered classroom supplies in September, it's now April. I haven't received even one new pencil. My students need books, workbooks, and art supplies. This school year is almost over. All of my school supplies have come out of my own pocket." I matched her stoic posture.

The assistant director seemed caught off guard. "Really? Let me check with the office staff and get back to you." She stomped away a bit louder than she entered.

I heard through the grapevine that the director and assistant director were being investigated on charges of embezzlement. Those classroom funds never existed. It was time to cut my losses and seek employment in the public school system where I belonged.

I turned in my resignation in June, 1985. The director had the nerve to attempt intimidation tactics, even in the light of his demise.

"You know, Jeaninne, you signed a contract, which ends in August. Legally, I could keep you to it and not give you the recommendation that you need for employment elsewhere." I wanted to slap that smug look off his criminal face.

"Well, sir, when it comes time to subpoena witnesses regarding your impending case, I will be the first in line to relay this particular conversation, coupled with the fact that I haven't received any classroom supplies for ten months." *Don't mess with a scorned woman*

This disgraced doctor of education accepted my signed resignation and reluctantly promised to give me the recommendation I deserved. I turned on my heels and never looked back.

Ben was laid off his construction job as the valley projects ended. I began a fervent search in the surrounding districts while Ben seriously pondered his fate. I decided to tip his scales toward a dream Ben had since childhood. His unhappiness chipped away at the hope of our marriage.

Six months before we left Park City, Ben's anger returned unexpectedly. Ricky, who was with me in that Santa Monica folk club when I met Ben, came to stay for the winter break. We skied during the day and enjoyed quiet evenings around the fireplace, reminiscing old times while Ben cooked for us. I often found B.J. sprawled across Ricky's lap when she read in bed.

Ben was laid off his construction work because of heavy snow storms, so he and B.J. enjoyed their cross-country skiing forays in the hills behind our home while Ricky and I enjoyed downhill skiing. We planned a pub crawl through the town of Park City for New Year's Eve, 1984, four months before our wedding and six months before our move to Nevada City.

Many young people in Park City arranged for taxis to town, then spent the rest of the night hopping from one pub to another on foot. I wanted to celebrate my best friend and my fiance in a festive atmosphere.

I felt Ben's mood shift when we were getting ready that night. He wasn't talkative with Ricky and became distant with me, only answering my questions with a yes or no.

"Ben, our first pub crawl. Won't it be fun to see our friends and new people celebrating the new year?" No response. Ricky and I checked our make-up in the hall mirror.

Ben eventually gave me a side glance smirk. Ricky joined in with her tawdry sense of humor, "Maybe I'll even meet someone and give you two some space to celebrate alone tonight." She gave us that sultry look that usually makes us laugh. I laughed. Ben rolled his eyes. *The darkness is back.*

I tried another tactic. "Well, at least the buffet dinner at the racquet club will be welcoming. After a few drinks, we'll be starving."

Ben quipped, "In the car, ladies. Let's get through this night as fast as we can."

Ricky and I exchanged concerned looks. *This is going to be a long night.*

Ben ordered a beer at the first pub. I thought this was a good sign, he was willing to loosen up. However, with each pub, Ben withdrew a bit more. Ricky and I drank two drinks during the entire evening. We felt high on everyone's celebratory energy. We left Ben alone at the bar so we could engage others in lively conversation. I knew better than to push him into a social situation when his dark side flared.

We arrived at the athletic center completely ravenous. Once we found a table, Ben slammed his keys down. "You drive yourselves home, I'll take a taxi." Without explanation, he disappeared through the back door. Several people stopped mid-bite and stared at us. I felt disrespected. *Was I a victim of public ridicule? How do I recover from this?*

"I'm sorry, Ricky, I just lost my appetite." Embarrassed, I lowered my head.

Ricky squeezed my hand. "It's okay, Jeaninne. We don't have to stay."

"No, we need to eat." I used every ounce of my dignity to hold back the tears during our meal. Inside the truck, I let my anger explode.

"I'm so sorry you had to see that, Ricky. Please know it has nothing to do with you being here. Ben likes you. It's me. For some reason, he has waged a passive-aggressive war on my personality. He reacts negatively to my optimistic ways. He doesn't seem to believe who I present. He resents my love for him. B.J. has been a huge lift in our marriage. We adore her and want the best for her. We work as a team for her. I haven't seen this behavior from Ben in a long time. I can't find the source of his anger."

Ricky, an experienced therapist, responded, "It appears Ben is reacting from unresolved issues from his childhood. You have told me things about his gregarious, alcoholic father who was hard on him during his adolescence. Maybe, you remind him of that time. I'm just guessing. It would take a therapist much time to help Ben look at his past and sort out some of his demons. You saw the possibility of those demons when you met Ben." *She's right. I did.*

We let B.J. sleep in Ricky's room that night so we could talk freely. B.J. picked up on every emotion we felt. If things weren't right between us, B.J. disappeared into another room.

"Okay, Ben, what happened? You left Ricky and I to weather everyone's pity as you stomped out of the lodge. I felt so embarrassed and disrespected." I steadied my voice because I really wanted to yell at him.

"I know. I know. It's just that I hate parties with people I don't know, they seem so contrived. With Ricky here, I didn't want to express my dissent because you two were so excited about going." Ben sat at the kitchen counter with his head in his hands. Now and then, he ran his fingers through his thick mane of auburn hair.

"It would have been better if you just dropped us off and picked us up at the end of the evening. But I was afraid to suggest that for fear you would think I didn't want you to be with us."

I saw the pain in his eyes, but it wasn't directed at me. It was pain that had come from somewhere deep in his soul, atavistic pain from a time long before I came along.

"I'm sorry, Jeaninne. I'll apologize to Ricky in the morning." He seemed like a shriveled, defeated, old party balloon that had lost most of its air.

Relieved that Ben didn't hold a grudge with Ricky, I made sure she enjoyed a few more days with B.J. and me. I accepted Ben's apology, but I never forgot how he could turn on a dime.

⌒

I was hired in August, 1985, to teach at a public middle school Special Day Class in Lincoln, forty-five miles down the mountain. Ben found a job deeper in the foothills as a counselor for teen boys in a court-mandated reform school.

Both of these jobs required much stamina, energy, and time. Two stressful jobs frayed the edges around our marriage. Even B.J. couldn't hold back the unraveling. Ben arrived home from work one evening with a look of defeat carved into the worry lines of his face.

I sat him down and asked, "What's wrong, honey?"

"I can't do it anymore." Tears formed in the corners of his eyes.

"What do you mean?" I couldn't imagine what had happened.

B.J. put her head in his lap as if she knew her papa was feeling blue.

"I can't be what those troubled boys need. I'm so torn up inside about their hard lives, I can't be tough. They take advantage of me. Maybe they remind me too much of myself when I was their age. So, I quit tonight."

He folded to the floor with B.J.

Ben pressed B.J. into his chest. She looked as crestfallen as he felt.

"Well," I said, "You tried. It wasn't a good fit. Why don't you think about pursuing your dream? It's time."

Ben returned to his chair, "You mean, apply to be a smokejumper?"

"If that's what it takes to make you happy. Yes." Ben wiped away his tears.

"You realize I have to go away for several months of training, then who knows where I'll be stationed."

His face searched mine for approval.

B.J. picked up on the energy shift of our conversation and came to my side. I kissed the top of her head and continued, "I can teach anywhere. Just get your training out of the way, then we can decide." I felt lightheaded with relief.

All the love we originally felt for one another flooded back. Ben, B.J., Boogers, and I gathered on our little yellow couch in a suspended moment of hope.

CHAPTER SIX

SMOKEJUMPER

Ben joined the Hot Shots fire squad after several weeks of training—a necessary requisite to be considered for the elite team of men and women smokejumpers, those brave souls who jump out of planes to accomplish initial fire suppression on wildfires that aren't attainable by ground vehicles. B.J. and I witnessed a new man. Ben came home excited about being in a wilderness career where he made a difference. I was proud of his tenacity and hard work.

Ben was often sent away to fires in and around Northern California as the Hot Shots were the initial line of ground suppression before large equipment and fire trucks arrived on the scene of a forest fire. B.J. and I spent many days alone. I jumped into my pursuits outside of teaching as long as B.J. could be by my side.

I actualized my passions outside of work. I became a talk show host for the community station KVMR. I wrote and produced my shows around timely teen topics like suicide, drugs, self-esteem, and current trends in music.

My show, "Teen Scene with Jeaninne," ran from 1986 to 1989. I also joined a community theater troupe and acted in three Nevada City plays. The dramatic arts consumed a huge part of my life in high school and college. Acting ran in my blood.

B.J. continued to be my number one. Knowing my days and nights would be filled with teaching, planning a radio show every week, and attending play rehearsals, I changed our running schedule. I ran with B.J. every evening for three miles after she spent each day with me in the classroom.

When it was time for me to leave for play rehearsals, B.J., exhausted from all-day kid care and our long run through town, was happy to be in the house with Boogers until I arrived home a few hours later. This busy schedule kept me from missing Ben and it satisfied my need to create.

B.J. became a part of me, like an extra arm or leg. I couldn't imagine being without her next to me while I went about my daily life. She linked me to Ben. I saw how she created magic for anyone whose life she had touched. I experienced B.J.'s potential while teaching at the middle school before therapy dogs became legitimate in the helping professions. B.J. healed damaged souls.

One such story defines B.J.'s positive effect on the most insecure of my educationally challenged students. John brought his puppy in one day to show the class. As he reached into the basket to present that little scraggly mutt, he announced, "I decided to name him B.J.!"

He beamed with pride. Nine months earlier, John didn't have a friend. He was on the edge of a crisis intervention. Little did we know, B.J. would become one of John's most effective mental health counselors.

I was amazed at John's progress, but B.J. was not. She instinctively knew a kindred spirit. When John enrolled in my class, he ducked in and out of the shadows of dark hallways, trying to hide his awkward, overweight body. Until he met B.J.

Already seeking professional help for John's depression at the beginning of the school year, it didn't occur to me to factor in B.J.'s effect on my students. However, when John saw B.J., he dove to the floor to be nose-to-nose with her. He giggled, then loudly exclaimed, "Look everyone, her eyebrows go up and down in opposite directions!" The rest of the children dropped onto the floor to see for themselves. Sure enough, B.J.'s eyebrows did teeter-totter, something I had never noticed before.

John didn't seek shadows quite so often after that day. My class surrounded John with friendship because of their mutual admiration for my golden girl.

B.J. made John laugh until he left us for high school, much thinner and more confident. I'd like to take credit for John's positive transformation, but B.J.'s love gave him reasons to believe in himself.

⌣⟶

When Ben returned home from the fire lines, we were like newlyweds. One evening, I suggested we go out on a dinner date to one of my favorite bistros. Ben preferred quiet dinners at home, but I wanted to celebrate his hard work.

He agreed because I think he grew tired of the many ways I prepared tofu, my latest health craze. I couldn't hold back my enthusiasm for showing off my handsome husband in town.

"It's so nice to be together again, Ben, tell me about the fires." I glanced around the dimly lit cafe looking for familiar faces.

"I know, I can't believe I'm finally home for a few weeks." Ben seemed genuinely happy. Just as I was about to listen to his fire stories, a familiar couple walked by our table. I recognized the gentleman from my radio workshops before we had acquired our talk shows.

"Hello, Jeaninne." An attractive silver fox with glasses gave me a nod.

"Hi, Jeff." I responded with a slight wave.

Before I could introduce him to Ben, Jeff and his wife had disappeared out the door.

Ben gave me one of his cold stares. "Who was that?"

"Oh, that's Dr. Jeff, he has a medical talk show on KVMR. We went through the same training class." My stomach lurched. *Ben, please don't make something out of nothing.*

"Hmm." I could feel Ben freezing me out.

"Are you upset?" *Jeaninne, why did you jump to that question? You are inviting a fight.*

"No. But, I don't have any idea what your life is like anymore." Ben looked pained.

"That's why we are catching up now, Ben." It was too late to save this evening.

"Eat up, I want to go." Ben fumbled with his wallet to pay the bill.

Ben remained aloof until his next fire. He ran with B.J. each evening to Scott's Flat Lake while I attended my aerobics classes. I was grateful that B.J. was back with her alpha male, but I cried into her soft coat each night before bed because I felt helpless against Ben's dark moods. We needed professional help.

I lost myself in my work and the radio show until Ben returned home a few weeks later from the fire lines. Only this time, something had changed.

I always waited for Ben with my stomach tied up in knots, not sure how I would be received. We started over after each work separation like a young couple in love, but something I said or did inevitably set him off, igniting his inner fury. On this particular homecoming, I didn't expect the person who entered the house.

"Jeaninne!" Ben banged through the front door and scooped me up into his arms. After three fast twirls around the tiny living room, he put me down and announced, "I'm in! I got accepted into the smokejumper training program!" I couldn't have been happier for him.

B.J. flew into Ben's arms from her corner of the couch. He twirled her around the living room, as well. At the dinner table, Ben told me everything.

"I'll be leaving for Alaska after the holidays for three months of training. After that, we'll be assigned to a home state for an indefinite period of time. It may be a few years before I get to choose my location. Are you good with that?"

His face exuded joy, how could I not be good with it?

"Ben, I'm good with wherever we land, as long as you're happy." I threw my arms around his waist. He kissed the top of my head.

Reminiscent of our first days together in Park City, nothing could stop us.

Our month together ended too fast. We ran with B.J. on her favorite routes around town and in the forested areas. We camped like we did when we first arrived in Nevada City, without any idea of where our lives might take us.

We loaded up our ski gear, with B.J. in tow, and hit the Tahoe slopes. We took turns on the runs so one of us could play with B.J. in the snow around the lodges. I was living the fantasy marriage I had imagined when I first met Ben.

Ben rented a motel by Lake Tahoe one weekend instead of driving the two hours down the mountain to our home. The three of us piled into the bubbly spa tub after a long day on the slopes. Then, we spent an hour blow-drying B.J.'s coat to keep her warm.

Ben treated me to a steak dinner at one of the nicest restaurants on the lake. I can't remember a happier time than the Christmas of 1987 before Ben joined the most elite of all firefighters. His dream became our reality.

Ben drafted a rigorous physical schedule to strengthen his lanky 6'3" frame, barely reaching 160 pounds before his induction date in January. He installed a chin-up bar on the front porch, hoisting himself up and down several times a day. B.J. and I accompanied him to all his workouts around the high school track—his private cheering squad. We clocked his sprints, counted his weight reps, charted his pull-ups, and laid on his back when he did his push-ups.

I even cooked comfort meals like spaghetti, tacos, and meatloaf. Ben "beefed up" to 175 pounds, still thin for most men his height, but acceptable for being a smokejumper. Thrilled he could meet the pull-up and push-up requirements for carrying 100-pound packs, Ben passed the all strict regulations. He could be dropped alone into wilderness areas, capable of surviving. I never doubted his abilities, even though he would prove to be one of the lightest, yet most tenacious, smokejumpers in the history of the organization.

Ricky came back for another holiday visit. Only this time, Ben made plans to climb Mt. Whitney, the highest mountain in California, for New Year's Eve. He realized that Ricky and I would have a better time celebrating in town without his disapproval. Ben learned that I would accept anything that gave him pleasure.

The visit went well, but we missed B.J. She opted for wilderness camping with her papa, which made Ben extra happy.

Ben came back with stories of spying on brown bears and catching fish in clear streams. I clearly imagined the fun they had. Ricky and I enjoyed our time skiing, shopping in local boutiques, and eating in bistro cafes. Ben and I learned how to compromise.

"You should have seen B.J., Jeaninne. She sensed an adolescent brown bear up the mountain, hidden from our trail, but kept her distance. I've never seen her instinct so keen. I could tell that she knew to respect wildlife, but she would've killed that bear, or died trying if that bear had approached me." Ben's body, charged with electrified static, hummed while he relayed their adventures. This was the man I married.

"Thank God, it didn't come to that, Ben. But I know what you mean. When we run in the evenings, B.J. stays close to me with her ears up, rotating at all times. She knows her job is to keep us safe. That's why I'm not afraid when you're gone. I'm sad, but not afraid."

Before Ben left for Alaska, he offered to build a few things for me that had been on my to-do list. I taught a particularly rowdy group of teen boys who lived in a neighboring group home. The district placed all of them in my Special Day Class because it seemed like the logical thing to do.

However, I needed to prove to my superiors that a current Individualized Educational Plan, or IEP, backed by extensive educational testing was the only way to enroll any child in my program. Until I could straighten out this dilemma, and get some of these boys where they belonged in the regular classes, I had to do something about their distracting behaviors.

B.J. knew how to deal with them on a one-to-one basis, but whenever I tried to give directions, they played verbal volleyball across the classroom. I implored Ben to help me figure out a way to keep them separated.

He had the perfect solution.

"I'll bring in plywood sheets and build study carrels. I can craft them such that one cubicle can seat two desks with a wall in-between." Ben's chest puffed with pride.

"That's a perfect solution! Thank you, honey." I felt like Olive Oyl hanging on Popeye's strong, tattooed arm.

One Sunday, B.J. and I kept Ben company while he built three huge cubicles inside my portable classroom. Six of my wildest boys finally had their own space. They even decorated their cubicle walls with artwork and posters.

None of the other students complained because the trade-off for a calmer classroom was the compromise to which everyone had agreed. I thanked Ben each day I returned from work for calming a situation that could have escalated into more stress than I could have managed.

Sadly, before I left the middle school seven years later for a new position in the district, I witnessed the maintenance staff hauling out the flat cubicles to move my old portable to a new location. The land upon which my first classroom sat was being allocated for the new elementary school that would eventually become the last teaching position of my career.

The day I returned to the middle school to load up my last boxes in June, 1994, I watched a maintenance truck speed away across the empty running track, dust flying everywhere. Ben's cubicles, which had become piled-up wood flats, were bouncing up and down in the truck bed.

B.J. and I walked to the field on the edge of the track to get a better view. I reached down and stroked her head. In her ear, I whispered, "I miss him too."

Ben also built us a bed before he left for his first training as a smokejumper. He spent a day in the forest above our town finding fallen tree trunks. I was amazed how he found eight perfectly matched logs in diameter to carve a four-poster bed by hand.

He spent hours shaving and cutting to get grooves notched into the smooth logs like a giant Lego project. Ben managed to fashion a log bed big enough for a king size mattress. That bed, too high for B.J. to climb, cradled us in his love. B.J. had her place underneath the bed on her mattress.

We did one more thing together before Ben left. We ran in a charity run around Donner Lake near the apex of the Sierras. Since Ben, B.J., and I had been running daily since we met, I knew I was up for the high-altitude, seven-mile run.

We trained together before the race, mixing up our daily runs to cover Ben's route and mine. It was also a good way for

Ben to further his smokejumper training. The last charity run I had raced was in Park City. At 8,000 feet, the 10K proved to be a challenge, but another runner stayed in my blind spot, to my right and slightly behind, setting my pace.

"Ben, remember that run in Park City when I competed with that other woman?" I clearly remember how much I relied on that woman to keep me going.

I was thinking of that day as I looked out of the truck window at the snow-capped Sierras on our way to Donner Lake. The sun directed its rays through the pine trees, its glow reflected off the snow fields that sparkled like fluffy white cake frosting.

B.J.'s breath chuffed over me as she stood on the back seat with her head out the window. Her saliva hit the side of my face. Heaven.

"I was doing so well in that Park City race until that woman suddenly stopped. I yelled back at her, 'You can't quit now!' She doubled over and waved me on. I finished, but with half a heart. I hope I can make good time today."

Ben looked at me. Smiling, he said, "You will ace it, with or without a pacer." His face projected kindness.

I felt loved.

"Thanks for your belief in me, Ben. It means everything." I reached back and high-fived B.J. She wore her perpetual smile; that bubble gum tongue hanging out the side.

Ben, a seasoned marathon runner in Alaska, finished the seven-mile Donner Lake run within forty-five minutes. He wanted to get back to B.J. waiting patiently at the start line with many other pooches tied to the shady park fence.

We debated whether to let her run with us, but decided it would have been too stressful for her. Ben would have had to constantly urge B.J. forward as she tried to double back to me, slowing him down in the process.

When the start gun exploded, I watched Ben shoot out from the pack of runners. He set his pace early, looking every bit like a world-class runner—white nylon tank, blue nylon short shorts accentuating long sinewy legs. I hung back to conserve my energy for the long haul ahead in my red nylon shorts, loose purple tee, and older Saucony running shoes.

I looked back and saw B.J. sitting straight as an arrow, straining to watch her owners doing what they loved. I blew her a kiss before I concentrated on downshifting my pace into a meditative state of pure running bliss.

The glossy gray lake that flanked my left side was outlined in the opulence of the slightly snow-dusted Sierras. I breathed in and out to the rhythm of my steps remembering our Park City runs in the Wasatch Range.

I prayed that we had vaulted over the final hurdles of our marriage. That day seemed to coalesce into our time as husband and wife. Even the other runners around me were caught up in the rhythm of my happiness; I didn't need to rely on another runner's pace.

As I neared the finish line, I heard Ben yell, "Go Jeaninne, you've got this!" I could see him pumping his fists in the distance, B.J. stood by his side with that pink tongue hanging out of her goofy smile.

Ben's cheers jump-started my adrenaline. I blazed through the finish line like a woman on fire. B.J. knocked me to the ground, covering me in kisses. The three of us felt like we could conquer anything as long as we accomplished it together.

CHAPTER SEVEN

MARRIAGE

The day Ben left for Alaska remains a jigsaw of memories, some pieces larger than others. I hate goodbyes, so I've trained my mind to erase the details of a parting as soon as a loved one leaves. I have blocked out much of the crying and desperate emotions between Ben and me on that particular day. Yet, I distinctly remember B.J.'s reaction.

When Ben bent down to hug his girl, she had a faraway look in her amber eyes. She knew. Normally a calm dog, ever Zen-like, B.J. stiffened against Ben's chest. It broke my heart. She was already steeling herself for the pain she would feel in his absence.

Ben pushed away, grabbed his duffle bag, threw it in his Volkswagen truck, the one I drove up that snowy mountain pass in Utah. He looked back once before he pulled out of the driveway.

Memory is a fickle mistress. Sometimes it implodes and takes over the present of the moment with every sight, sound, smell, and taste, or the mind erases its existence as soon as the action occurs. Sometimes, it creeps back into our consciousness like a thief in the night—slow, quiet, fleeting— leaving a scattered residue of loss.

Ben's last look held one of those stealth memories. His piercing blue eyes, sheltered by a bushy auburn unibrow, filled with tears. The descent of those tears accentuated his high cheekbones and perfectly sculpted nose. He half-smiled through full lips framed in a groomed beard.

I watched Ben comb his hand through his thick hair before he drove out of sight.

B.J. and I spent our days filled with teaching and daily runs. I continued my radio show and added a part-time job teaching aerobics on the weekends. Being busy was an antidote for missing Ben. Time became something to mark until our alpha dog came home after three months of training. I waited for each letter with bated breath, reading each one out loud to B.J.

Looking back, it was more romantic not to have the technology of emails, texts, or screen time. Ben's letters and phone calls were enough to keep our love alive.

I returned home from work later than usual one evening. After a long faculty meeting, I didn't get home until sunset. B.J. was anxious to run, she endured close to two hours in the car because of an accident on the freeway. I needed to get her out for a run and home before dark. Just as B.J. and I were stepping through the front door threshold, the phone rang.

"Hi, it's me." Ben sounded good.

"Hi Sweetie, B.J. and I were just leaving to get a run in before dark. I had a long meeting, then we hit traffic from an accident on I-80. How's training?" My body was itching to move.

"Busy. We've been practicing our jumps all week as I wrote about in my letters. I've landed my jumps within the target zone each time. I don't think the other dudes expected this skinny guy to keep up." I heard the pride in his voice.

"Oh, Ben, I'm so proud of you! Listen, B.J. is hopping around by the front door and it's getting dark. Can I call you back?" I was anxious to be back before dark.

Silence. *Uh oh. I blew it.*

"Ben…" *Please speak.*

"Uh no, not necessary, I should grab some grub and hit the hay. Don't worry about it."

Click. *Oh shit, he's upset.*

Dark thoughts clouded my mind as B.J. and I ran through town. She stopped in front of me so I wouldn't run into a car turning in front of us. I sensed Ben's anger before I hung up the phone. I called him all week, but he only had access to a pay phone in the jump shack. Each time I called, his unit was out in the field. Waiting for his next letter was excruciating because I feared his wrath.

I felt the content of his letter before I opened it. Shaking, I ripped into the envelope.

> *Dear Jeaninne,*
>
> *You obviously don't miss me. I could tell by your voice from our last phone conversation that you just wanted to get on with your evening. I'm sorry I interrupted. I'm now wondering if you just wanted me to become a smokejumper so you could move on with your life. I know I seem negative, but it's what I feel.*
>
> *Love, Ben*

I stared at that letter for what seemed like an hour. I'm sure it was only for a few minutes, but I was in a mild state of disbelief. I couldn't fathom that Ben had arrived at such an extreme assessment of my character. I mean, he knew how much B.J. and I needed those runs. He knew I had to drive forty-five miles each way to a stressful job, and that our daily run was how I alleviated that stress.

I had sacrificed our marriage so Ben could follow his dream. Yet, I was the bad guy. For the first time in our relationship, I was no longer sad. I was pissed.

I wrote Ben an angry letter and then waited for his call.

"Hi," was the only word I could muster when I picked up the phone.

"Hi." Ben seemed distant. "I'll be coming home this weekend for a few days of leave."

"That's great because we need to talk." I could be distant, as well.

"Yes, I know." He never mentioned my anger.

I didn't know what I felt when I hung up, but I could see in B.J.'s face that she wanted an answer. Her eyes were searching my face for any news of her papa. I couldn't resist the hopeful joy expressed through her wagging tail, feather dusting the floor.

"Yes, Beej, Papa is coming home. It's time we settle a few things." Then I wrestled her to the floor, knocking into Boogers, who was cleaning her paws and minding her own business.

Prepared, I waited for Ben's icy demeanor when he walked through the door.

"We need to try counseling if this marriage is going to survive. I won't have you blaming me for all of it." Even my stance was strong; I wouldn't back down.

Ben leaned in for a kiss.

"Okay," he said. Ben removed his jacket, hung it on the hall tree, then set his bag down by the door.

B.J. waited patiently for her welcome, sitting on her haunches between our stand-offs. She could feel the intensity of our greeting.

We exhaled together before Ben bent down to B.J., allowing her to lick him until his face was completely wet. B.J. knew how to elicit the basic part of our love, bringing us together.

76

We agreed to use a referral for a marriage counselor in Auburn from one of the psychologists at work. We decided to take a weekend trip to Carmel-By-The-Sea, then drive further north to Mendocino, before we embarked on marriage counseling. I knew it would be a healing start if we could be together without the stress of our jobs interfering.

Ben packed up our camping gear with a renewed spirit. B.J. followed Ben's every step as he arranged the car. She loved her car trips and would prove to be my trusty companion along the entire state of California for many years to come.

Before we left, we stocked Boogers with plenty of food and water, secured her cat door, and battened down the hatches. We drank several cups of coffee with the anticipation of driving the scenic roads that lead to the Pacific Ocean, only a few hours away.

Whenever I drive to the coast, I imagine my life as a California Indian before the Spanish explorers arrived. Ancient Oak trees blanket the rolling Coastal Range with gnarled branches, reminiscent of the witch hands illustrated in popular fairy tales. With massive trunks and perfectly rounded silhouettes, the branches reach out, bending dramatically to the ground, once cradling the early people who relied on them for shelter and acorn meals.

I can drive for hours seeing Indian villages in my head. In my mind, the asphalt road disappears and I become one of the indigenous women gathering seeds, picking fruit, and chopping fire kindling as my children romp over the land, their laughter echoing off the hillsides.

That day, I looked at my stoic husband driving through this wonderland, then back to my sleeping girl, content to daydream about the indigenous Californians without a worry in my head.

With an eighth of the California Pechanga tribe pulsing through my veins, these fantasies carry even more weight in my imagination. My ancestors play key roles in my musings whenever I drive the California coastline.

Driving out of the hills into the coastal canyons is also a spectacular experience. On one side of the highway, the hills appear large and imposing; on the other side, the end of the earth drops off in a long stretch of sheared cliffs, brutally sliced by seismic activity. The azure-blue Pacific Ocean spreads as far as the eye can see.

Each time I happen upon this visual banquet, I imagine wooden galleons with multi-layered canvas sails carrying Spanish soldiers and Catholic priests on their way to conquer the Americas.

I put Ray Ban sunglasses on B.J. for this particular trip because the sun's heat bounces off the ocean and ricochets back in a blinding light. She didn't knock them off for the duration of the trip.

Other drivers delighted in the sight of B.J. in sunglasses, her regal head sticking out of the back seat window, hair feathers blowing back from her face. Her healthy pink tongue, accentuated by that black dot birthmark, flapped out of her smiling mouth. That moment, still vibrant in my mind, captured her complete and utter joy to be on the road.

We spent the first night in Carmel. Ben and B.J. ran on the protected beach cove while I strolled through the Carmel village stores right out of Hans Christian Anderson's Denmark—tiny shops replicated to look like thatched roof troll dwellings. We stayed in a dog-friendly bed and breakfast inn, complete with a fireplace and kitchenette.

B.J. found her spot in front of that crackling fire after we dined in a dog-friendly patio restaurant. She didn't move from her warm position until we packed up the next morning for the fishing village of Mendocino.

This is where Ben shone. We found a campground at the foot of the forest that spills out onto Highway 1, the road that hugs the coastline along the full length of California. Ben set up the tent while B.J. and I hunted for firewood. B.J. delighted in finding sticks longer, and almost as thick, as her broad body. Before the sun set, we walked down to the rocky beach, dodging the crashing waves and jumping over rock formations.

I watched Ben and B.J. becoming silhouettes on the craggy shoreline against the dying light of the day—Ben's long and lean profile with B.J. at his side, loyal and loving. I snapped a mental picture of that scene not knowing how long this fleeting serenity would last.

The rest of the trip culminated into a slide show of images that clicked quickly through my mind—bike rides, dinners on the beach, playing in the surf, campfires around our tent. Ben and I chose not to talk about the future. We simply wanted to become reacquainted. Even our lovemaking was easy again.

However, on the way home, we felt reality seeping in through open car windows with each passing mile. Ben turned off his words. B.J. no longer stuck her head out of the window. My chest tightened, my heart raced, and my breathing became shallow by the time we drove into Nevada City.

The elephant of our relationship was no longer in the room, it crashed through the front door and was sitting on top of our car before we even entered the house.

"Now what?" Ben asked. His vacation calm had seeped out of his body.

"What do you mean?" My calm was replaced with dread.

B.J. was on the porch touching noses with Boogers who had already come out to greet us.

"I only have a week until I go back to Alaska. Do we really need counseling?" *The elephant spoke. He wanted us to battle for our marriage.*

"That's what we agreed upon, but if you want to wait until your next leave, we can see how the rest of our time together unfolds. I'm so afraid of being blamed again when you're away." I stared him straight in the eyes without blinking.

Ben ignored my concern. "Let's enjoy the rest of the week until I leave." We left it there.

⟋

B.J. and I met Ben in various Nevada locations when he was transferred from Alaska to Colorado in the spring of 1987. I packed up my Volkswagen Golf to drive over the summit of the Sierras with B.J. as my co-pilot.

Belted beside me, B.J. concentrated on the road. I looked into her calm face, wondering what she was thinking. My driving soliloquies, delivered out loud, consistently centered around one sentiment:

B.J., you're my best friend, my perfect child, my wise teacher. I don't know what I would do without you. Thank you for navigating this unpredictable life with me. Mommy loves you very much.

Sometimes, we stayed in a Reno hotel along the gambling strip, but most of the time, we stayed in funky motels in places like Lovelock and Winnemucca. Ben and I talked along the trails of our desert hikes about the possibility of having children.

"Ben, I don't feel comfortable about this until we seek counseling." Walking side-by-side felt like an easier way to approach this conversation.

"I don't feel comfortable about counseling at all. Why do we need it, anyway?" My chest tightened when Ben announced this concern.

"Because you still pull away from me after a long absence. I don't feel secure enough in our marriage to bring in a child right now." There, I said it.

"Is it someone else?" Again, that icy stare.

"No. I can't believe you asked me that! This is precisely what I'm talking about." My heart pounded hard against my rib cage.

"Why else wouldn't you want a child, Jeaninne? You're already thirty-three."

"I do want your child when we know where your permanent base will be." *What am I afraid of?*

We continued our hike focusing on B.J., not uttering another word the rest of the way.

Ben's next visit home was the following summer. We finally agreed to try for a child. Excited to have him home, I begged Ben to take me to the Nevada County Fair. I thought some fun time together was just what we both needed to refresh the marriage. Ben could be much too serious. Part of his attraction to me was my feisty spirit and the enthusiasm with which I approach everything in life. Ben reluctantly agreed.

While walking down the midway between the arcade games and the kiddie rides, I noticed a booth buried in a variety of hanging stuffed animals. I grabbed Ben's arm and exclaimed, "Oh, Ben, win me a stuffed animal!" I wanted him to be my hero that day.

Ben walked on without response.

Nope. Not today, Ben.

"Please…please?" I linked my arm through his, leading him back to the booth. "Why won't you answer me?" I felt Ben's body stiffen.

A deadly shot of adrenaline blasted through my body, feeling like a sniper's bullet had hit me from out of nowhere. A strong force propelled me to the ground.

Ben had cupped his hand around the back of my neck, pushing my head downward.

The shock of this was so sudden, I couldn't speak. Dozens of fair attendees stopped in their tracks.

I broke free just before my knees buckled to the ground, and then I ran for my life!

Ben followed me, but I outran him until I reached the truck in a distant parking lot.

Through my panting sobs, I screamed, "Why?! Why would you physically humiliate me in front of a crowd?! I just wanted you to be my hero. I can't do this anymore."

Ben hung his head and let the tears fall, begging for my forgiveness.

"Jeaninne, I swear, I don't know why I did it." I didn't want to hear his excuses, I just wanted to keep running.

"Please listen to me, Jeaninne. It's not you. It's me. I guess my anger gets the best of me when I feel pressured. I know it has to do with my childhood. I know my parents love me, but when my father drank, it was hard on all of us. I learned to stuff my feelings away."

Ben wiped his tears on his sleeve.

On his knees, Ben pleaded, "Can we go home now?"

The only response I had came out quick and cold, "Only if you watch me make an appointment for counseling when we walk in the door."

I reluctantly hoisted myself into the front seat.

⌣⌐

"Ben, you seem uncomfortable." The therapist caught on to his reluctance.

"I don't want to be here, but I know I have to for our marriage to survive."

Ben sat with his arms crossed against his chest.

"Jeaninne, tell me why you're here."

The words burst out of my mouth. I relayed the county fair incident in every detail.

"Ben, why did you force Jeaninne to the ground?" The kind doctor leaned forward.

"I just felt pressured to win her a stuffed animal. I don't know, but I suddenly felt trapped and angry beyond my control." Ben shifted positions.

"Did you communicate that to Jeaninne before you acted so aggressively? Do you often react this extreme?" The therapist pushed his glasses up on his head.

"No, that was the first time I have ever snapped like that. I guess I just let things build up. It's hard for me to talk about my feelings. I feel so ashamed and bad for Jeaninne." I felt compassion for Ben, even though I was still angry.

"Jeannine, do you pressure Ben to do things he doesn't want to do?" I had to think about that.

"I don't think I do, but I can be overly emotional and somewhat demanding."

"What do you think about that, Ben?" Ben's eyes softened when he looked at me.

"I suppose Jeaninne's emotional ways are hard for me."

"And why is that?" The therapist leaned back in his chair, giving Ben space.

Throughout our first session, the doctor led Ben to his past, sensing that my natural ebullience represented something deeper and more symbolic for him. Ben touched upon the fact that his father was effusive and charming when he drank. The session ended with a promise that we would return the next week. We did.

"Jeaninne and Ben, thank you for returning. After tonight's session, I would like to see you individually before we begin the marriage issues. Would that be alright?

"I'm in," I said.

Ben nodded. However, I felt the opposite behind that affirmative nod. I feared he had closed up for good.

The following week, I attended alone. We delved into an overview of my father's leaving us for another family when I was eight years old, and the dynamics of my blended family at the time of my mother's second marriage when I was twelve. The therapist wanted a full picture of our separate lives to navigate how Ben and I related as a couple.

Ben attended one time by himself. After his session, he said, "I can't do it. I can't talk about my childhood. I can't betray my parents. And even though my father was hard on me when he drank, I know he always loved me. "

That was that.

We limped along with B.J. in the center of our tumultuous marriage. When Ben came home in between assignments on the fire lines, we concentrated on doing B.J.'s favorite things— running, camping, swimming.

Ben never lost his temper with me again. I felt he was deeply remorseful about the neck squeeze; nevertheless, we became strangers. Even our love for B.J. couldn't hold our sadness at bay. We knew the marriage was over, but neither could take the first step. We loved one another, but love wasn't enough to bridge the differences in our personalities, nor the pain in Ben's tortured soul.

One greeting card ended it, once and for all.

CHAPTER EIGHT

CHUCK

Time is like a hologram, if you try to contain it, you are left with an illusion of your making. Looking back, I wish I could have avoided certain ways of handling my marriage—taking more responsibility for my part in Ben's unhappiness and being swayed by people I wish I had never met at the time when my marriage hung by a thread. I yearned to turn back time to the night I met Ben.

Charles was one of those people who came along at the wrong time. A fellow teacher who snared me in his charismatic fantasy net, Charles caught me when I had been bobbing in a life raft from a sinking ship. During the worst time of my marriage, his friendship felt like my life preserver. Freezing and desperate, I grabbed onto Charles in the middle of a dark, raging sea of fear.

Charles, better known as Chuck, seemed like everything Ben wasn't. Outrageously creative, zany, unconventional, and brilliant, Chuck compared to no one I had ever known. He made me laugh all the time. Nineteen years older than I, handsomely weathered like the Marlboro man, Chuck's hero status with his three teenage children became the shiny object that fascinated me.

As a single father, he elevated his children above all else. I subconsciously wanted some of that fatherly affection to rub off on me as my dad had cut ties when I was eight years old. Chuck and I were destined to collide in one way or another, for good and bad.

Our friendship started at work. During lunch, we spoke of similar interests such as books, movies, art, education, and the vicissitudes of life. Since Ben and I weren't laughing much, I looked forward to a few minutes of levity each day. Chuck listened to me. I expressed my fears, not knowing what to do about my failing marriage.

The spark between us crept up like two elementary students walking home from school, sharing secrets sealed with a spit shake. Chuck even babysat a few of my behaviorally challenged students for an hour in his shop classes each day. He became a true friend when I needed one most.

Chuck lived on the lower two hundred acres of the four hundred acres he and his family owned in the Lincoln foothills. He often had after-school socials around a campfire on a creek flowing downstream of his double wide mobile home.

Because of Chuck's Peter Pan outlook on life, he never actualized plans to build a permanent home for his family. Chuck preferred living in a teepee next to his trailer when his children were young. I saw this aspect of his personality as boyish and charming, blinded to the reality that Chuck lived in a fantasy world of his own making.

B.J. romped around the cattle land that Chuck's family leased to neighboring ranchers. She learned from her scare in Park City with that crazy dog, Moose, to stay on the periphery of the grazing herds. B.J. carefully navigated around the cows to arrive safely at the small lake on the other side of the property, where she could chase ducks and geese to her heart's content. B.J. and I often broke away from the creek socials to run, marveling at the magnificent oaks that dotted the hillsides. I reveled in feeling like the indigenous people who lived simple lives off the land. B.J. and I ran freely across those vast acres without a care.

While my friendship with Chuck was budding, Ben rarely came home for visits. As a fully-fledged smokejumper, he lived suppressing wildfires. It would have been career suicide for Ben to turn down any jobs. I understood that.

We spoke daily on the phone, wrote letters, and promised to work on our marriage whenever he did come home. I remember that this time in my life was bittersweet and lonely. I know B.J. felt it, too. She never left my side.

Teaching kept me busy, but weekends without Ben were interminable. I wrote in journals about the chipping away of our marriage, the evolution of my grief. I don't know how many times I cried on B.J.'s head, leaving her wet with my tears. My four-legged girls became the reason I got up each morning. B.J. lived her life to make me happy; Boogers brought me dead birds and live garden snakes through the bedroom window as tokens of her love. I leaned on my furry family to get me through the loneliest days of my life.

In late August, 1988, a few days before teachers had to be back on the payroll preparing for the new school year, Chuck asked me to accompany him to San Francisco for a day trip.

He needed to drop off blueprints to some Bay Area artists for custom waterfalls he hoped to build when he retired. Ben didn't like big cities, so we never enjoyed this spectacular city together, even though it was only a three-hour drive from the foothills. I didn't listen to my better instincts and accepted Chuck's invitation. A part of me knew that Chuck wanted to spend more time with me. I wanted to have fun and forget about my woes for one day. Of course, B.J. had to come or the deal was off.

Much of that day in and out of dog-friendly restaurants and beautiful parks has dissipated from my memory because I couldn't stop thinking about Ben. However, B.J. and Chuck had fun diving in and out of the surf after we accomplished his waterfall business.

I didn't bring a bathing suit, but I was happy to oblige B.J.'s passion for swimming. I agreed to extend our day for more time on the beach.

"Jeaninne, let's stay until the sun sets. I know you want to get home for Ben's call, but how often will you be able to see the sun set behind the Golden Gate Bridge? These are the moments that make life worth living." I tried to ignore Chuck's desire to be romantic, but a part of me loved the attention I had been lacking.

"You make an argument that's hard to refute. I never tire of watching B.J. glide through the water. Look how happy she is." Her glorious face could have easily been a golden seal's as she sliced through the choppy water, sparkling like diamonds. I cherished that look of bliss whenever B.J. lived in the moment.

Chuck put his hand over mine and said, "I would like to see you as happy." My heart jumped a beat before I pulled my hand away.

"Hopefully, Ben and I will be happy again." *What am I doing here? I need to be home to get Ben's call.*

"Or, maybe your happiness lies elsewhere." Chuck's perfectly weathered face framed by a full head of white hair looked like a billboard advertisement for living the good life in California. The setting sun behind him framed the outline of the iconic Golden Gate Bridge.

I was taken aback by the directness of his comment. "At this point, I don't even want to think about tomorrow. We better get going." *What is happening?*

I called out for B.J. and wrapped her in a beach towel before she could roll over and over in the sand, bringing much of the beach home with her. I felt relief for this perfectly timed moment of diversion. By the time we walked back to the car, B.J.'s damp hair felt silky dry. We drove home in a comfortable silence, commenting every now and then on the highlights of our perfect day.

Once we returned to Chuck's ranch, I still had an hour's drive up the mountain to Nevada City. I needed to get home and my anxiety showed in my nerves. I put B.J. in the car after she ate, drank water, and did her business. As I started the ignition, Chuck leaned in my car window and handed me a blue envelope.

"What's this?" I knew it was something I shouldn't take.

"Don't read it until you get home. Just my way of thanking you for being you. And, thank you for coming with me today, it made my errand much more enjoyable." His impish blue eyes twinkled.

"Well, thank you for giving me a respite from my sadness, B.J. and I had a great time. See you at school next week." I couldn't get out of there fast enough.

I watched Chuck wave goodbye through the rear view mirror, and then I looked ahead to concentrate on the dark country road that stretched into an uncertain future.

⌒

B.J. and I walked through the door at 11 p.m. Boogers was happy to see us. She and B.J. shared their day via the hindquarter sniff fest before they settled into their spots on the couch. I noticed the flashing light on the answering machine.

I felt my heart banging against my chest when I played it back. "Well, you must be busy. I'll call again in the morning when I can get to the jump shack phone."

I sat on the couch between my girls to catch my breath, worrying about Ben's thoughts. And then, I remembered the card. I pulled it out of my canvas bag and carefully removed it from the blue envelope. It was a blank card with a picture of the sun dipping below an ocean horizon.

> *Dear Jeaninne,*
>
> *You are the most dazzling woman I have ever known. Thank you for your friendship and for trusting me as a friend. I only want the best for you, whatever that is now, or could be.*
>
> *Love,*
> *Chuck*

This friendly note came with a grenade of emotion. If Ben found this, it would be our demise. I buried it outside under all the trash at the bottom of the dumpster. I didn't rip it up because a tiny, irrational part of me wondered if I should retrieve it and hide it in a more secure spot. Or, maybe a subconscious part of me wanted it to be found. In the following days before Ben's return, I forgot all about it.

CHAPTER NINE

GOODBYE

B en surprised me on the cusp of the new school year.
Busy preparing my classroom and attending mandatory
meetings a week before the children were scheduled to begin
classes, he called me at the school that morning to tell me he
hitched a ride with another jumper from the airport earlier than
expected. After the last meeting of the day, B.J. and I raced
home to see him. Chuck and I had exchanged pleasantries that
week at work, but nothing more was mentioned about our day
in San Francisco. Chuck respected the fact that my husband
was coming home.

Everything changed on that hot August day in 1988.
I couldn't wait to hear about his stories from the fire lines. I

especially enjoyed learning about Ben's brave parachute jumps into a smoldering area of the forest that could potentially become a raging wildfire.

It thrilled me to imagine my husband carrying a 100-pound backpack filled with fire-retardant devices, an aluminum pup tent, army rations, and a medical kit. I imagined his tall, muscular body encased in a yellow jumpsuit as he floated through the sky, sometimes entangled in giant pines and firs.

He would throw off his heavy pack, untangle his parachute lines, and then rappel down the tree, wasting no time hacking away at burning timber with an axe. My husband, Ben. My hero.

When I drove into the long driveway, I immediately noticed the manicured lawn, the freshly planted marigolds at the base of the wrap-around porch, and the smell of something delicious wafting through the front door screen. Ben stood on the porch with a distorted smile.

"Wow!" I exclaimed. "You've been busy?" I ran to him with open arms.

Ben greeted me with a stiff hug. I grabbed him back, not letting go. Ben dropped to the ground with B.J., like he always did when he was away too long.

He stood up and said, "I wanted everything to be nice." It felt as though an alien had hijacked my husband's body.

"What's that smell? It's heavenly." B.J. and Boogers circled our legs, excited to have Papa home.

"Listen, can we talk before dinner? I made a stew with all I could find in the fridge, it may take a while." Ben's face remained stoic as if carved in stone.

I stuck my hands in my jean pockets to quell the shaking. "Sure. What's on your mind?"

In the minutes that followed, my life changed forever.

Ben led me into our spotlessly clean cabin house behind the old Victorian—the home where we met Aleasha and Kevin; the home where I began a new teaching career; the home that encouraged me to take on my own radio show, act in community theater, and teach an aerobics class; the home where B.J. learned to accept a fenced-in yard; the home where Boogers brought us nature's gifts; and, the home where Ben found his true calling.

He sat me on the yellow, faux leather couch and held Chuck's blue envelope in front of my face. Everything around me blurred, except that damn card.

With that stare that could bore through steel, Ben said, "Explain."

Forcing myself not to crumble into despair, I begged. "Chuck is just a good friend. He makes me laugh. I needed some comic relief from missing you for months at a time. He feels more for me than I for him. I have drawn those lines. Please believe me."

He didn't.

Ben walked into the kitchen to prepare our last supper. I followed him to help. He refused to say another word. We ate in silence.

I fed B.J. and Boogers outside so they wouldn't feel the pain that had filled the tiny cabin like a deadly gas.

Ben packed a few belongings while I washed the dishes. He finally returned to the living room with a large canvas bag in one hand and a medium-sized backpack in the other.

"Here's the deal: we each have four thousand dollars in savings, so you keep your money and I'll keep mine. You keep everything in the house, sell my mountain gear in the attic if you need extra cash. I'll find a place in Auburn until I know my next assignment." That impassive stare never blinked.

I've often read about how humans react to a devastating experience—disbelief transforms into physical numbness; the brain pumps an abundance of adrenaline, protecting the body from a sudden shock to the nervous system. Words screamed in my head, but nothing came out. Stunned into silence, I was paralyzed with grief.

Ben walked out the front door. The screen door banged in my head like the explosion of the Hindenburg blimp.

I jumped up and ran after him. B.J. followed.

As he slid into the front seat of his truck, I pleaded, "What about B.J.?" I already knew I couldn't live without her. She looked confused, staring at Ben, then back at me.

He smiled, "She has always been your dog. I can't take her to the fires." Ben reached down and ruffled her soft fur as he did when we first brought her home.

Again, I pleaded. "We need to talk. This can't be the way it ends." I was hanging on to anything that would make him stay.

"I can't. Not now." Ben wouldn't look at me. He started the engine, slowly backed out of the long driveway, drove up the hill, and then disappeared around the bend. B.J., Boogers, and I stood frozen on the grass. If I moved, then it would all be real.

I finally walked back into the house and cried for hours, my head buried in B.J.'s silky golden fur.

I ached from the questions reflected in her sad eyes, *"Where did daddy go? Is he coming back?"*

CHAPTER TEN

DEPRESSION

For a year after that heartbreaking day, my life became a broken 16mm movie reel stuck on a continuous loop. I could have taken one frame and played it over for 365 days to describe my life after Ben. In essence, I would have watched a sad, thirty-four-year-old woman with her equally sad, five-year-old Golden Retriever commuting to the valley from the Sierra foothills and back, stumbling through a quick evening run, and then falling into bed by 8 p.m. The weekends consisted of long blank frames of nothingness marked by loneliness. At least B.J., Boogers, and I had each other.

Having to teach at-risk teens and caring for my girls saved my life. Depression was the only feeling I could count on.

Some days, I prayed to God to take me in my sleep. I felt like such a failure. However, each morning my golden girl rested her face next to mine from beside my bed. She never whimpered or barked before I awoke; she waited patiently for me to open my eyes.

B.J. knew I needed her near. She used her love to keep me from giving up. She gave me hope. I learned to put one foot in front of the other.

Depression became a constant companion that respectfully stayed out of my way when I needed to get on with my life. Enough can't be said about the rallying support of friends and family. So many people surrounded B.J., Boogers, and me throughout this difficult time.

After Ben moved to a rental in Auburn, he was dispatched to Boise, Idaho. I saw him one more time before he left Northern California. But, he didn't see me.

On a late Friday afternoon, two months after Ben left, I drove home on the back roads of Lincoln. The golds and reds of the October leaves, framed under a royal blue sky, stole my breath—one of those brief moments of glory I savored to get me through the never-ending sadness. B.J. sprawled across my lap as I drove through the twists and turns of Highway 193. She had her mourning to master.

When I approached the last stop sign before merging onto Interstate 80, I glanced over at the Park and Ride parking lot. My mind lagged a few seconds behind my brain: Ben and Chuck were standing face-to-face. I had already accelerated into the merging lane once the realization of seeing them together kicked in. I cranked the car around onto the shoulder, barely missing an oncoming vehicle, and then I screeched back into the parking lot.

Chuck leaned against his car with his head down. I jumped out of the car like an escaped felon.

"Was Ben here? Where is he?" I whipped my head in every direction, searching for Ben.

"He just left." Tears ran down Chuck's face.

"What did he say?" I wanted to shake the whole scene out of Chuck.

"He wanted to know if I was in love with you. I couldn't answer yes or no." Chuck looked painfully confused.

I strapped B.J. into the back seat and drove home as fast as I could. I ran into the house and called Ben.

"Why didn't you tell me you had planned to meet up with Chuck?" I barely caught my breath.

"I needed to know the truth without your interference." His voice sounded flat, emotionless.

"Can we meet up tomorrow and talk?" Again, I begged.

"No, I'm leaving for Boise tonight." He was done.

"Ben, we need to sort this out. I'm not done with our marriage. Chuck is mistaken about our friendship being more." *How can I make him believe me?*

"It's not about Chuck anymore. I'm ready to move on. I guess I needed any excuse."

We spoke only a few times after he settled in Idaho. Once, during a huge forest fire in Nevada County, Ben called to see if I was alright. I implored him to meet face-to-face, but he dismissed the topic. The second time, during one of my mother conversations, Ben happened to be at her house in Southern California.

"Mom, are you alright?" I can always detect the slightest change in my mother's voice.

"Uh, yes, why do you ask?" She is a terrible liar.

"Mom, what's going on?" I wouldn't let her slide.

"Ben is here." I knew it.

"Give me the phone." *Don't do this to me, Mom.*

"He won't speak to you." *Oh, so you are on Ben's side.*

"Give me the phone, please." By then, I was crying.

"Ben is here to say goodbye to me. He's upset because he swears he saw you and Chuck together in your car driving through Tahoe City before he left for Idaho."

Oh my God, she can't believe that's true. It's Ben's paranoia and jealousy!

"Mother, you know I haven't seen Chuck, except at school, since Ben left. Please put him on the phone." I felt the hysteria of my anger exploding in my head. I heard my mother coaxing him to the phone.

"Ben, I haven't seen Chuck outside of work since you left. Why would I lie?"

"I don't know, Jeaninne. Listen, I can't talk anymore. I was leaving for my sister's when you called. Give me time to process everything; we'll talk later." *I don't believe you, Ben.*

Our marriage was over.

B.J., never far from my side, had leaned into me during the phone call. I crumpled to the floor and wrapped my body around her.

She didn't move a muscle while I sobbed into her back. Boogers had burrowed into me with her back to mine. My girls. My reason to be.

I called Chuck over the weekend to inquire about his encounter with Ben. He sounded far away, a shell of the man I thought I knew.

"How did this come about, Chuck? I mean, why didn't you warn me?" The lump in my throat made it hard to breathe.

"Ben called me. I could hear the pain in his voice. He made me promise not to involve you, a man-to-man thing." *Men and their stupid alliances.*

"What did he ask you to do?" I couldn't imagine.

"He wanted to see my face when I spoke of our friendship. I thought that was fair." *Chuck, a good man.*

"Did you tell him we are just friends?"

Please tell me you did.

"Ben is an honorable man. He would have seen that what I feel for you is more complicated. I can't talk anymore. I have to go."

Click. *How did it all come to this?*

I wouldn't see Chuck, apart from passing him in the hallways, for four more months. He was battling his fight with Bipolar Disorder, a depression far worse than Ben's.

B.J.'s PROMISE ~ JEANINNE ESCALLIER KATO

110

CHAPTER ELEVEN

SURVIVING

Summed up on one page, the divorce symbolized the brevity of our marriage. I picked up the form at city hall on the advice of a lawyer. Since we were childless and shared neither money nor property, this was the logical course of action. Ben didn't contest it when I sent him the form for his mandatory signature. The marriage officially ended on October 29th, 1988.

The letter I wrote to my friends and family proved harder to navigate. Sitting in the kitchen at the pine table on my Macintosh computer while B.J. looked up at me with those soulful eyes, I banged out my feelings. I wrote to my loved ones that our divorce was a painfully mutual decision due to irreconcilable differences.

I emphasized that we would hold one another in the highest regard, and we would cherish our memories. I included our love for B.J. as a highlight of our union. I wondered if Ben would ever see B.J. again. Sadly, he never did.

I kept my commitments to teaching aerobics and producing my weekly radio show, "Teen Scene with Jeaninne." My creative pursuits helped to heal my broken heart, but B.J. gave me the impetus to move on. Because of her, I got up each morning.

When a journalist came to the house to do a story on my radio show for the local newspaper, I wouldn't participate in the interview if B.J. couldn't be in the picture with me. She inspired me in all things. I thanked God each night and each morning for her presence.

I learned that being a woman alone made our lives more vulnerable.

Summoned to report for jury duty not long after the divorce, I couldn't take B.J. to school that Monday. I prayed she would be safe in the backyard with plenty of water and shade until I was scheduled to be home before 5 p.m. Relieved that my jury group wasn't selected, I raced home to my girls. Only Boogers greeted me.

Before I turned off the engine, a neighbor from up the hill appeared at my driver's side window. She breathlessly explained that B.J. had been wandering the neighborhood like she used to before we fenced her in. When she saw the animal control truck stop in front of my house, she flagged the officer.

She pleaded to keep B.J. in her yard until I got home. He would have none of it. The officer suggested she relay his message: I could retrieve my dog at the city pound in the morning after I paid expired license fees. My neighbor begged the officer to let her watch B.J. No deal.

I cried hysterically while my kind neighbor told her story. I hugged her, ran into the house, fed Boogers, and then I called every civic number I could think of to locate someone who could release B.J. immediately. Thinking of her being afraid and alone all night in that cage made me nauseous.

Every office had closed for the day. I did the only thing I could. I drove to the pound in Grass Valley to see if a security guard could help me.

The parking lot was empty. All entry doors were locked. I noticed the cyclone fencing around the back and heard the loud wails of a dog in distress. When I found B.J.'s nose pressed through the wire fence, I howled with her. We kissed and cried together for an hour.

I promised B.J. I would be back first thing in the morning. Walking away from my baby that evening was worse than the year of sadness I had just endured. Through my tears, I could barely see to drive.

I abandoned my girl.

At dawn, I called the district substitute line to arrange for a sub. I wouldn't go anywhere until I could get B.J. back into my arms. I didn't sleep at all. I saw B.J. sitting at that wire fence, shaking and sad.

I imagined her thoughts: *Why did you leave me, Mommy? Are you going away like Daddy did?*

I stood first in line the next morning.

B.J. squeezed through the open gate and jumped into my arms. I cried from joy, exhaustion, and relief. "Mommy loves you, sweet girl," I whispered in her ear. I quickly paid the fees and swept my girl into the car.

"Okay, Beej. Today is your day. What should we do?" B.J. plopped a paw into my hand, staring happily into my eyes.

"Scott's Flat Lake it is!" I drove B.J. home first to make up a picnic basket, including her favorite treat, Ol' Roy peanut butter dog biscuits.

Nothing comforted me more than to see my girl swimming in wide circles with that goofy grin on her face. It was even worth bringing home a dirty, wet dog. I rewarded her with a warm bath and a night of cuddles.

"Where were you today?" Chuck's call came as a surprise.

Even in the retelling of B.J.'s ordeal, I couldn't contain my tears. Losing her scared me more than anything.

"Were you able to fix the fence?" Chuck sounded genuinely concerned.

"Unfortunately, there are places along the ground where B.J. can push through. Since this is a rental, Ben couldn't put up a permanent fence." *Damn that landlord.*

"I can come up this weekend and drive in some better stakes. I'd hate to have you go through this again." I exhaled for the first time in two days.

Chuck offered a safe haven. I accepted.

B.J.'s PROMISE ~ JEANINNE ESCALLIER KATO

CHAPTER TWELVE

REBIRTH

Chuck's friendship was like being pulled out of a dark well, my drenched body placed into the sun. Since Ben refused to look back, I had to do the same. Chuck was good to B.J. and me, and it was a relief to have a man's helping hand. B.J. could be left for short stretches in a secure yard, thanks to Chuck's ability to rebuild the fence. He proved instrumental in other ways that helped me move forward.

Chuck often drove up to Nevada City for weekend visits, but his sprawling ranch in the flat lands became B.J.'s paradise. She swam in the creek by his double wide trailer, chased little critters, basked in the sun on the banks of the lake, and ran the periphery of the land with me by her side.

Chuck could never replace Ben, but B.J. appreciated his unique lifestyle. Ultimately, B.J. wanted me to be happy.

Winter had arrived when we started dating, often snowing in Nevada City. With Ben, I never drove in the snow because of my horrific experience with that one drive in Utah on Parley's Canyon. As a single woman, I was determined to learn how to put snow cables on my tires. I needed to drive in case of an emergency, no matter what the weather dictated. My decision to install cables without help proved to be a lifesaver on the first snowy Saturday of the winter season.

I had no idea that B.J. licked up antifreeze from our driveway while I was focused on figuring out the installation instructions.

Once I finished the job, I drove into town to test my work. B.J. seemed fine when I left her in the house with Boogers.

After returning from my two-mile trial drive, I noticed B.J.'s strange behavior. She seemed drunk, but I quickly realized she had ingested something chemical by the metallic smell of her breath. I threw her in the car as her muscles began to spasm. I drove to the nearest veterinary clinic as fast as my cabled tires could take us. My body downshifted into emergency mode. I didn't even realize that I was driving on a snowy highway with compromised visibility.

The adrenaline surging through my body forced me to focus only on B.J. After the on-call vet pumped her stomach, keeping her on fluids all day, she finally stabilized.

The veterinarian patted my shoulder. "You brought her in just in time." I felt eternally grateful I pushed myself to install those cables. I wanted to call Ben and tell him that I had finally earned my mountain woman status. Reality dictated that would not be wise. Ben made it clear he had moved on.

As a single woman commuting an hour each way to work, I felt more vulnerable to things that could go wrong. I never thought about my health, but for my girls, I worried all the time. Boogers, a Siamese mix, had a strong constitution. Except for summer flea infestations, she stayed healthy until her passing at age eighteen.

On the other hand, B.J. presented me with enough vet bills over the years to cover a down payment on a substantial house. Being a purebred canine, and not having her specific bloodlines on paper, I didn't know the genetic disorders that would plague B.J. later in life. However, I learned quickly how susceptible her delicate skin, under that red silky hair, was to foxtails.

Chuck hosted a summer barbecue on the creek to celebrate the end of the 1988-89 school year. B.J. swam in the creek and rolled through the dried fields, redolent in foxtails.

We didn't get home until midnight. I spent an hour brushing out hundreds of foxtails embedded in her coat. For a few days that followed, B.J. continuously shook her head and licked her paws. Upon closer inspection, I saw the red, swollen track marks between her paws, under her arms, and in her anus. I couldn't get close to her ears or she yelped.

"Oh, baby, Mommy is so sorry you are suffering, but we must get these out or they will burrow into your body and cause major health issues." My stomach heaved at the sight of too many track marks.

B.J. plopped her paw on my knee as if to say, "Thank you, Mommy."

I hugged my girl and whispered, "I would sell my soul for you."

CHAPTER THIRTEEN

Dr. Laura

B.J. needed surgery to extract those insidious foxtails. It wasn't the surgery that upset me as much as her neglectful care. The attendants from a clinic in Grass Valley brought out a dog I didn't recognize—B.J. smelled sour and shook uncontrollably. I cried at the sight of her. Instead of the angry outburst I should have performed, I expressed my dissatisfaction to the staff in hushed undertones of rage. I'm sure they put her in a cage and left her there without any post-care attention. B.J. healed from her wounds, but it took me weeks to heal emotionally from her traumatic post-op treatment. Thankfully, fate arranged alternative plans when I wasn't looking.

My mother came for a visit after B.J. recovered. I had been feeling the desire to leave the house I shared with Ben, but didn't want to ruin our visit with any talk of the divorce. Seated in a coffee shop one morning, my intuitive mother picked up the newspaper left by a previous customer and read some of the want ads.

"Jeaninne, here's something you might consider: *a mother-in-law cottage for rent on a local horse ranch. Call Dr. Laura at the Mother Gold Animal Hospital.* Wouldn't it be nice for B.J. and Boogers to have a veterinarian as their landlord? It might be healing for you to start fresh with new memories.

You should call right now and inquire before it's taken. Let's go home and do that before we go shopping." My mom wouldn't give up until I called. We shared an understanding of unrelenting instincts.

Within that week, two people advised me to relocate. My childhood friend, Maureen, mentioned that it might be time to start fresh in a new place, just as Ben had to move away to get on with his life. My mother knew me better than anyone; her advice came wrapped in unconditional love.

I called the number and made an arrangement to see the place the following week. As life often interrupts our best laid plans, destiny directed my meeting with Dr. Laura sooner than our previously scheduled appointment. Scratching B.J.'s belly the day after my mother left, I noticed that her vagina was red and swollen.

I knew it must have been another foxtail that had burrowed further into her body, a foxtail that awful clinic missed. I also noticed that she had been obsessively licking her lady parts, as dogs do when they attend to open sores.

"Well, Sweetie, we might as well meet Dr. Laura now. I promise I won't take you back to any place that would mistreat you. This time, you'll have a proper woman doctor who understands your lady bits and keeps your dignity intact."

B.J. looked at me with her appreciative, loving gaze, the one thing I counted on each day. Whenever I looked into her soulful brown eyes, I always felt comforted that my worries would become my solutions.

A blonde apparition in a white coat floated into the examining room. As in the magic of Hollywood, I saw feathered wings and fluffy clouds circling this woman who could have easily become a professional model instead of a doctor of veterinary medicine.

Even B.J.'s ears perked up when the stunning Dr. Laura walked in the room. She smelled like lilacs in springtime.

Dr. Laura bent her 5'10," voluptuous body down to B.J.'s level, exclaiming in a voice that could have belonged to Snow White, "Who do we have here? You are a beauty, B.J. Let's see what's wrong, Sweetie. I promise I'll be gentle." B.J. melted into Dr. Laura's long arms. I made the sign of the cross and closed my eyes in a thankful prayer.

"Doctor, thank you for seeing B.J. before our appointment to see your rental. I knew this nasty foxtail couldn't wait. B.J. recently had a bad experience with foxtail surgery."

I told her about that nightmare clinic and the suffering B.J. and I endured.

"First, call me Laura. And second, I'm already in love with B.J., so if you like the house, it's yours. Yes, this foxtail is too far up the urethra to pull it out with a probe, but I can assure you B.J. will be cared for by every staff member as if she were the hospital's dog. B.J. is in great hands."

I could have kissed her angel face. Within an hour, I had a new home and a new doctor for B.J. and Boogers. I grabbed Dr. Laura in a bear hug, feeling like she lifted the weight of the world off my shoulders.

Laura hugged me back. "Welcome to the family. When you pick up your sweetheart tomorrow, we can arrange a visit to the rental. And make sure you say hi to my Schnauzer, Tybo, on your way out. He will be B.J.'s new buddy." I bent down and kissed B.J.'s nose. "B.J., you even have a built-in friend in our new place!"

I walked out of Mother Gold Veterinary Hospital with a feeling of joy I hadn't experienced in a long time. I knew my baby was being cared for properly and I had found a home for me and my girls. July,1989, the month and the year I moved on from a sad divorce.

CHAPTER FOURTEEN

HORSE RANCH

Chuck's curiosity for my new place piqued when I told him about Laura's horse ranch. At the end of a long gravel road off a narrow highway between Grass Valley and Colfax, Laura's modest red ranch house appeared on a slight rise above five acres of manicured horse pastures. Most of the surrounding properties were at least a few acres.

The Arabian horses grazed contentedly within those pastures that stretched as far as a football field from the main house. Trails led from the house down to Rollins Lake behind the property lines. The city girl in me felt like she may have bit off more than she could chew, but she was willing to choke on a few pieces of hay to make it work.

Chuck and I could start over as a couple without being in Ben's shadow, even though a part of me would never forget the happy times with Ben, nor the pain of a failed marriage. In my prayers, I wished Ben well. Enough time had passed to give me a healthy perspective of what went wrong between us. We weren't a good fit.

Huge Ponderosa Pines rimmed Laura's home and the pasture lands, so I didn't see her mother-in-law cabin until I drove around to the side of her house. The coffee-colored cabin sat at the bottom of the gravel driveway in its own little valley facing the barn. Even smaller than the Victorian back house in Nevada City, it still felt right.

This square cabin in the woods housed a tiny living room, bathroom, kitchenette, and bedroom. The picture window in the living room framed the giant Ponderosas dotted around the red barn in the background. The small bedroom, just off the corner kitchenette, included the north-facing window from where Boogers could slip in and out.

I envisioned her hunting in the Manzanita brush and pine trees. I felt like Gretel without Hansel, following bread crumbs on a solo hike through the never-ending woods of my life.

Laura already passed my inspection for the doctor my girls deserved. When I retrieved B.J. from the hospital, she was sparkling clean, not cowering in the corner of some neglected kennel. Laura said her foxtail was an easy removal with a remote chance of infection. The office staff and vet techs sent B.J. home with hugs, kisses, and antibiotics.

"Okay, girls, you and Boogers need to help me start packing because Dr. Laura is our new landlord. We are in for the journey of a lifetime, but first we have to move out of our old life." B.J. laid her head on my shoulder from the backseat of my Volkswagen Golf, still groggy from her procedure. With her by my side, I knew I made the right decision.

Back at the Nevada City house, B.J. followed me from room to room, watching my every move as I methodically boxed up my belongings. I could feel her anxiety rise with mine as I thought about all the good and bad times with Ben. With each item removed from the wall, I imagined her thoughts. Her eyes never wavered from my actions. I sensed B.J. knew her life was about to change.

I had one more bit of business to accomplish before Chuck arrived with his truck. I needed to go through the attic and sift through Ben's mountaineering boxes.

I didn't have any energy left for the memories that last day on Nursery Street, so I picked out a few things I knew I could sell or donate—two cramp-on picks for ice climbing, an expensive sleeping bag, and a new pup tent. I looked at the rest of the boxes marked *Ben's Stuff* and said to myself, "I don't have the energy for this, let the new renters have it."

The day Ben left, I offered to give him the stained glass window Ben's sister made for our wedding, but he insisted I keep it. To this day, whenever I write in my office, I look at that stained-glass Cypress tree teetering on the edge of an ocean cliff. It makes me think fondly of our trips to the coast and of the gratitude I have had for every aspect of my life.

The tiny crack that runs across the right corner is also symbolic of a union that wasn't meant to be, but of a dog that was. Sometimes, things are not just things. They are tangible proof of our existence, priceless reminders of our worth.

⌣⌐

Chuck called to tell me he would be delayed a few hours with his ranch responsibilities. Relieved for the time left in the Nursery house alone to reflect upon my old life, I needed to say goodbye to Aleasha, Kevin, and all the other neighbors who watched out for B.J.

So many of my friends and family visited from Southern California over the five years in this house. Proud of the life Ben and I had carved out of nothing, I so enjoyed sharing the beauty of Northern California's Gold Country with loved ones. I walked around the Nursery house, giving homage to each wall, thanking that modest dwelling for keeping us safe.

We made quick trips for most of the day, back and forth from Nevada City to Grass Valley, transporting my belongings to Laura's ranch. B.J., completely distracted by the sights and smells of Laura's ranch, seemed to forget to grieve her previous life.

Tybo greeted us with his stumpy tail wagging on overdrive. B.J. and Tybo sped off to the barn like two school children up to no good. Boogers sniffed inside and outside of the cabin before she settled into her spot on the bed.

Chuck helped me arrange my furniture and break into important boxes. I treated him to a take-out dinner on the floor, boxes piled everywhere. We toasted with paper cups filled with cheap champagne.

Chuck left me alone to unpack and arrange the cabin without distraction. I told him that I wouldn't be at his ranch for a week so that I could acclimate my girls to their new lives.

Since I still had the summer to settle in, I wanted to do it right for all of us. Underneath one of the boxes, I found a welcome letter from Laura.

Dear Jeaninne, B.J. and Boogers,

Welcome to the ranch! I assigned Tybo the job of being the official greeter as I have to work late this week. Enjoy settling in, and if you have a chance, visit all my animal friends in and around the barn. I'm sure they will become your friends in due time. You might see, Judy, the neighbor down the road to the right, coming and going to take care of the horses. Please introduce yourself. We will catch up sometime this week.

Fondly,
Laura

B.J. and Tybo sat like bookends on the porch with the silliest grins on their faces, each holding a large stick that didn't fit on the porch. I laughed as they jockeyed around, neither one backing down.

I dug around in a box for the dog biscuits, giggling, "Best friends already, huh? Okay, you two, here's a snack. Now, get out of here and let me unpack."

After a few hours of unpacking, I couldn't contain my curiosity—*What other friends has B.J. met?*

I unlatched the gate to the barn and stepped into Laura's ark. Two pigs, whose names I later learned, Sara Lee and Jimmy Dean, rooted at my legs. A shy deer hung back, but seemed to want my attention because she lurked in my shadow all day around the cabin. That special deer, Johnny Doe, was attacked by stray dogs. Laura rescued her and repaired her reproductive organs.

A couple quarter horses nudged the hay bales, so I broke off a few bites to keep them from butting my backside. Playful goats romped around the enclosure. Of course, nothing could match the grandeur of the majestic Arabian horses grazing in the side pasture under the rays of the late afternoon sun. We were home.

B.J., Boogers, and I enjoyed that summer on the ranch. B.J. learned to stay around the periphery of the two houses with Tybo tagging along. They didn't venture down the gravel road to the main road, alleviating any worry that they would get hit by a car.

I drove nine miles into town to do my grocery shopping and teach my aerobics classes, expecting B.J.'s happy greeting each time I drove into my parking spot between the barn and the cabin.

B.J. and Tybo understood not to slip under the fences to disturb the horses. They even respected Johnny Doe's space when she nibbled on the savory ground cover around our porches. B.J. memorized the three miles we ran every day down the gravel road, east on Highway 174 to the Chicago Park Store, but she knew not to trot down that road without me. However, one stormy day changed everything I trusted regarding B.J.'s instincts.

Dark clouds hung heavy and low the Saturday morning I squeezed in my errands before the impending storm. Driving into my parking spot after an hour away from the house, B.J. did not appear to greet me. I called her name, but only Tybo obeyed.

"Hey boy, where's B.J.?" Tybo sat statue still, staring into me, but he didn't look like his usual, ebullient self. I heard a loud crash of thunder, Tybo ran to the barn. My body filled with dread. B.J. hated thunder.

I ran into the house to find Boogers safely curled up on the back of the couch. I noticed the flashing light on my answering machine before I dashed out to look for my scared pup. I played the message back because instinct alerted my senses that this call might be important.

Hello, I live off of Highway 174. I'm calling
because we have your dog, B.J. We found your
number on her dog tag. Please call as soon as you
get this message.

I felt dizzy from the blood rush of relief, immensely
grateful I had the sense to update B.J.'s ID with our new phone
number. I called back barely able to contain my emotions. My
hand shook as I punched in the numbers.

"Hi, this is Jeaninne, B.J's owner. Thank you so much for
calling me right away. I just got home, so I can come get her
now. It must have been the thunder, she hates thunder. B.J.
never leaves our property."

The kind neighbor said, "We had our door open because we
are in the process of moving. Suddenly, this beautiful Golden
Retriever runs into our house and dives under the bed, she was
shaking violently and we couldn't coax her out."

"She was looking for me; I am so thankful you had your
door open." I wrote down the directions and raced to my baby.

When B.J. heard my car, she ran out of the house and dove
into the back seat, bypassing any hugs and kisses. B.J. shook
like Aspen leaves in a strong breeze. I locked her in the car
while I quickly hugged those neighbors for their kindness.

Tybo met us in the driveway, excited to be reunited with his best bud. I let them sniff their hellos, yet I didn't let go of B.J.'s collar as the thunder continued. I spent the rest of the day cuddling on the couch with my girls, comforting them through the ominous storm, and listening to the rain pelt on our aluminum roof.

After that day, B.J. accompanied me for every errand; and, if I had a special event that prevented her attendance, I kept her in the house with Boogers or left her with friends who loved her. I had nightmares about driving home and never finding her for years to come.

Laura showed up on my doorstep one Saturday morning. "Jeaninne, I'm so sorry I haven't been available to you, I've been swamped at work. Thank you for keeping an eye on Tybo when he can't accompany me to the clinic. He and B.J. are quite the pair. By the way, I adore what you've done with this place." I invited her in for coffee, regaling Laura with the delightful antics of our cherished pups, the stories she missed. Our laughter felt healing and warm, like drinking sunlight.

The ranch life suited me well, even though my relationship with Chuck sailed on rough seas. I truly enjoyed my time with him, but problematic swells became crashing waves on our figurative love boat.

Chuck preferred not dealing with day-to-day life, so if we were romantically having fun, he was on board. Whenever I wanted to talk about our future, he shut me down with excuses and diversionary tactics.

I also found out that in fifteen years of being separated from his wife, he didn't file for divorce. She had already moved on to a permanent relationship. Chuck's aversion to commitment put an end to any kind of permanence for us. Our relationship would go through many changes until it became a life-saving friendship.

CHAPTER FIFTEEN

LAKE TAHOE

B.J. and I found our paradise on the North Shore of Lake Tahoe. We spent many memorable times skiing and bike riding around the lake with Ben. A small, rocky beach just south of Tahoe City fit our needs perfectly—a U-shaped cove for swimming and sunbathing with a minimum of distractions.

After our move to the ranch, I wanted to reward B.J. as a way to thank her for her continued loyalty. Each time I loaded up the VW Golf with towels and picnic baskets, B.J. bounced around the car and rolled in the red dirt. It was a refreshing way to get out of the sweltering heat that is common in the Northern California summers.

We had a ritual. I spread out the towels, filled her water dish, then made B.J. wait in sit position, her eyes dutifully locked on mine. When I said, "Go!" she raced to the water, dove in with a hearty splash, then swam in slow, measured strokes beyond the little breakers.

I dove in the water with her, but she had no interest in splashing around the shoreline with me. B.J. wanted to paddle past the weekend swimmers where she could glide in wide circles, watching the tourist boats to the rhythm of her own breathing.

On one of our outings, B.J. swam so far out, I panicked. I called and called, but she wouldn't come. She became a speck on the horizon, moving in a vast body of black, bottomless water. I left my belongings on the towel and swam out to her. She looked over and gave me that enigmatic smile, that smile that implied, *Trust me. I got this.*

"Yes, I know you love your lake swims, Beej, but you're coming back with me. I don't like you out this far in frigid water for too long. Let's go." I looped my fingers through her red woven collar, dog-paddling her back to the shoreline.

To diffuse her disappointment, we played fetch with a long stick along the water's edge. I packed up early that day. Fate warned me that too much of a good thing can be too much of a good thing. If I had allowed it, B.J. would have stayed in the center of that lake all day.

We often stopped at the marina to eat Tahoe's best deep-dish pizza at Lakeside Sports Bar. That day, I sat on the patio overlooking the wharf, feeding B.J. a few bites of pizza crust. She set her gaze on the dock where two black Labrador Retrievers dove for Frisbees.

"Sorry, girl, you've had your fill of the lake today. The most important thing in my life is your health and safety. I couldn't bear losing you. It's getting late, B.J., let's go home."

⌒

Things between Chuck and I reached an impasse. His pattern of evading a relationship became further complicated with his clinical Bipolar Disorder. I saw an ember of this firestorm when Ben left.

Chuck spiraled into a reclusive state after Ben confronted him about our friendship at the Park and Ride lot. I couldn't reach him by telephone for months.

At work, he barely spoke to anyone. Rumors circulated that he had "gone to ground" for a whole year when his wife left years before we met. At the time, I assumed he wanted to give me space, but the story dove much deeper.

Chuck's pattern of living in two extremes began to surface. As long as we could play in getaway places along the coast in a bubble of romance, he was upbeat and fun.

However, if I asked him to participate in real relationship activities, such as spending time with his family or attending events I enjoyed, he became evasive and emotionally unavailable. I began to make alternate plans with B.J. and new friends. I even dated. I lost hope that Chuck and I could be more than good friends.

I asked Chuck to accompany B.J. and me to a late summer 10K run in Truckee, a small town at the summit of the Sierras. Chuck declined, so I booked a room in Tahoe City for the Saturday night before the race. I wanted to be fresh for this difficult run that would challenge my physical stamina. I would be competing with the best, so I had to be at the top of my game with respect to sleep and nutrition. I didn't need Chuck's support as long as B.J. was with me.

"Okay, Beej, it's just you and me this weekend. We're going to our beach spot before an early dinner to the finest restaurant in Lake Tahoe. I packed your water toys and your favorite scarf."

Someday, I'll find a man who will put us first, B.J. We deserve it.

B.J. rolled over and over on the pine cone covered ground outside of our cabin, expelling a burst of gleeful enthusiasm. She jumped up and danced around Tybo. He joined in B.J.'s dance, yelping out his approval.

"Oh Tybo, I wish we could take you, but your mommy needs you here. Be a good boy; we'll be back on Sunday." B.J. jumped into the car grinning from ear to ear, barking back at Tybo. Their friendship gave me such pleasure.

I walked into the elegant restaurant that night like a lake queen with her golden princess. In my little black dress, strappy sandals, and silver jewelry, I led B.J., wearing a red scarf over her brushed, shiny coat, through the dining room.

The maitre'd had already secured a place for B.J. on the patio because I dropped off her portable bed and water dish when I made the reservation earlier that day. Her things, neatly arranged against the glass slider, looked as though she belonged there. I sat at a candlelit table for two in the center of the room facing my girl on the patio. The diners must have pondered the back story of the single woman with her dog in the middle of a romantic restaurant on a Saturday night. With B.J., nothing seemed out of place.

Back at the hotel room, full on fish, rice and vegetables, I luxuriated in a steamy bubble bath while B.J. focused her attention on cable TV animal shows. We turned in early, but I couldn't sleep. Loneliness seeped back into my life. I wanted a relationship I could count on; consequently, my thoughts strayed back to what Ben and I could have been. I reached down to pet my sleepy girl, thankful we were destined to share the same journey.

"I'm so sorry you lost your papa, B.J. He loved us fiercely, but his demons would not allow him to be happy. I know he would want us to be happy. Night night, sweet girl. Mommy loves you. Tomorrow will be a big day for both of us."

In a Truckee café the next morning, I loaded up on a huge protein breakfast for the 10K mountain run. B.J. lounged under my table. She ate her Science Diet kibbles in the hotel room, but I ordered her a side of scrambled eggs for being my support canine. Registration started at 8 a.m. I wanted to be fueled up and ready to go.

Because of the steep terrain laid out in a switchback pattern up and down the mountain, I chose not to include my girl. The trails were narrow and susceptible to injuries. There would be hundreds of runners trampling over one another in those narrow lanes, and some of us could even tumble down the mountainside. B.J. would wait in a secured, grassy dog area set up by the sponsors. After I registered and pinned on my paper number, I made sure B.J. could see me at the start line.

If I had known that a majority of the runners would be wearing state-of-the-art athletic clothing—light, shiny, polyester blend running pants with matching tank tops— designed to absorb sweat and repel the elements, I wouldn't have shown up in a white T-shirt and cheap purple running shorts. *Well, Jeaninne, enjoy your run, you may be bringing up the rear.* I waved to my girl, waited for the 9:00 a.m. gunshot, and took off in a leisurely stride, allowing the elite runners to accelerate around me. I conserved my energy for the harder terrain.

One of the allures of being a runner is the spiritual state of being in the zone. Once the body finds its natural rhythm, the mind is free to meditate. This amalgamation of body and soul, an elixir of adrenaline, deep breathing, and lactic acid, is akin to a higher level of consciousness espoused by Buddhist monks. I achieved my own Nirvana that day. The veil over my third eye was lifted.

"One foot in front of the other, Jeaninne. One, two, three, inhale. One, two, three, exhale." I repeated that mantra over and over until my body became nothing but a moving energy of emotions. Reels of scenes from my marriage projected in front

145

of my mind. With each step, a new scene flashed up. I watched a series of silent films, highlighting my face and reactions to Ben's actions. I saw that I was forcing myself to be happy by forcing Ben to be someone else. I didn't love Ben the right way. Our marriage failed because we failed equally in it.

We broke through the thick trees and reached the switchbacks. Runners flowed around me until I was alone on those narrow trails, pumping my legs, heel toe, heel toe. The sun, blazing directly over my head, had crept up from the east behind my back. Time meant nothing.

A bald, rail thin man was among the last of the runners I encountered on the side of the mountain. As he passed, he lightly brushed my back with his hand, and said, "You alright?" I smiled and waved him on. From that small act of kindness, the floodgates of my sadness broke open. I couldn't see the trail through my tears, but I felt free.

"Oh Ben, I'm so sorry I wasn't a better wife. I tried to make you happy, but it didn't work. I wanted to be the right woman for you, I really did. Forgive me. I should have been better. You are a good man. B.J. and I miss you very much, but we wish you well, wherever you are." I wiped the final tear with my arm and refocused on my pace. The sun lost its strength. I pushed to complete the race before everyone working the finish line left.

By 12:30 p.m., I was one of the last runners to cross the finish line. The outside folding tables were gone, and most of the runners, who weren't in the school auditorium milling around the snack tables, left the premises. I ran to my girl waiting patiently in her grassy enclosure; we rolled around on the ground as one body.

The volunteer smiled at me and said, "B.J. was the perfect guest. We spoiled her and gave her extra treats."

B.J., the enchantress.

I hugged the volunteer. "Thank you so much for watching my girl! I may have been one of the last runners, but I feel like a million bucks!!"

I completed 6.2 miles to the top of a mountain in the mighty Sierras—no easy feat. I felt as though I won! I released much of my guilt to be fully present. Even better, I shared this elation with my golden girl who waited patiently for me, confident that I would I always return to her.

CHAPTER SIXTEEN

SINGLE

B.J. and I spent time with Chuck on his ranch whenever the weather was too extreme for me to drive back and forth from the foothills. I appreciated having a refuge close to work. B.J. felt comfortable with Chuck in all phases of his brilliant mindset; whether he was reclusive or the life of the party, he always had time for B.J.

On cold afternoons in the dead of winter, Chuck cuddled with B.J. in front of his pot belly stove, the only source of heat in his rustic mobile home perched on an elevated rise of land above Coon Creek. This same creek is where Chuck raised his children to swing from tree ropes into the flowing waters that originated from the Bear River. If I couldn't reach him when he disappeared into the darkest recesses of his tormented mind, B.J. laid her head in his lap while he stroked her head. When Chuck really needed his space, he whistled for B.J. to walk with him to a small lake that rimmed the lower two hundred acres of his family's land.

Whenever Chuck hosted last minute parties, he was at his best. He loved being the host, the centerpiece of the action, because no one could spin fantastic tales like Chuck. B.J. followed him everywhere, knowing he would feed her bites of his sizzling, dripping meats hot of the barbecue. She was mesmerized by this man.

A part of me wanted to see if there was some way we could work things out, even though I knew Chuck wasn't my ultimate person. Whenever Chuck drew so far into himself to the point that even B.J. couldn't find him, I created a separate life in the foothills.

Laura often invited me to business mixers in the Grass Valley community where I met other accomplished single women. I enjoyed various fund-raising events so I could dress up and feel like an adult in contrast to the arduous responsibility of herding children all day.

I enjoyed riding on Laura's coattails as she was well-known, respected and wickedly fun. Laura tried to set me up with various men, but I quickly learned we were from two distinct political parties. I had nothing in common with conservative men. Laura teased me about my liberal leanings, "You're never going to meet a wealthy treehugger, Jeaninne." True. However, my life has never been about money.

The one and only time Laura introduced me to a liberal man was on the slopes of Squaw Valley. Laura and I laughed all day on the slopes, but the guy she invited to come with us turned out to be a potty-mouthed teenager in a grown man's body. That Neanderthal peppered the f-bomb between every other word. No way to impress a teacher in her late thirties. I had fun teasing Laura.

"Where did you find this guy, Laura? He's an idiot." We set him free on the previous run. We stood away from the highest chairlift surveying our mountain top trail options.

"So sorry, Jeaninne. He's a friend of a friend. The only liberal I know."

"You are adorable, Laura. I love you for trying, but don't ever set me up again. Definitely not your forte." She pushed me into a snow bank.

I couldn't wait to get back to my girls, the true loves of my life. However, Laura and I laughed all the way home.

Where I did find men with whom I could relate was at the local pub, Mad Dogs and Englishmen, in Nevada City, and through community theater. Each weekend, rock, blues and jazz bands headlined from the greater Northern California area.

One of the bartenders happened to be a KVMR disc jockey, a well-loved British colleague of mine. If I didn't have any plans with Chuck or my girlfriends, I would sit at the bar and spill my guts to Tony about my on-going soap opera with men.

Tony had been battling Juvenile Diabetes for most of his life. I had heard from the grapevine around the studio that he was not doing well. People born with diabetes endure a life of complications if they don't keep to strict diets, exercise and medications.

I didn't know Tony's complete medical history, but his fellow disc jockeys constantly worried about him. His friendly presence gave me the confidence to listen to great music without feeling as though I were a desperate woman alone in a bar.

It felt natural to sit alone and share stories with Tony regarding our work for the radio station. Tony laid the ground rules about not wanting to get involved romantically because of his health issues. His friendship was immensely more valuable.

I met two potential significant others at the pub. Rich, a strikingly handsome Spaniard from San Jose, ten years my junior, worked in the digital world of Silicon Valley. He came up on his motorcycle for weekend visits to see his family and me. I didn't envision a future with him because of our age difference, yet Rich never gave it a second thought. He was wild about B.J. I accepted that he lived too far for a true relationship, but I enjoyed how he filled in the lonely hours of my weekends.

I learned early on that Rich was torn between me and an ex-girlfriend in San Jose. I eventually persuaded Rich to follow his feelings and return to her. However, Rich did one thing for me that I will never forget—he stepped in and whisked me away from an awkward situation with another potential significant other named Larry. Rich helped get back my dignity when I needed it most.

I had just ended a budding relationship with Larry when I met Rich. Larry, a local architect, pursued me the old fashion way after we met at the pub one Saturday night. He kept smiling at me from across the room. Flattered that a handsome man signaled to me, I still refused to engage. When I finally rose to leave, Larry approached and asked me to join him at his corner table.

"I'm sure you noticed me staring at you. My name is Larry. I'm a local architect." I appraised his stocky 5'11" frame, dark blonde hair and brown eyes. Not bad. I detected a bit of arrogance.

"I did notice your gaze. I'm Jeaninne, a not so local teacher, but local disc jockey on KVMR." I'm sure he was appraising my 5'4" thin frame, long curly hair, and bouncy personality.

We chatted for a half hour more about the community of Nevada City before I said my goodbyes. I still wasn't sold, but I gave him my phone number.

The moment I walked in the door to hug my girls, the phone rang.

"Hello Jeaninne, this is Larry. I just wanted to make sure you got home safely. That road is pretty dark at night." *Nicer guy than I expected.*

"Thank you, Larry. You are an officer and a gentleman. I'm impressed."

"Can I call you sometime for coffee?"

"Sure, why not?" *What could it hurt?*

We began dating, but something seemed terribly amiss.

Larry wasn't totally present when he was with me. I decided to give him more time to see if the problem was real or imagined.

We enjoyed our dates. Larry even allowed B.J. to come with us if we were hanging in town or at his house, a stately Victorian situated on the banks of a river that ran through town. He eventually invited me to one of the biggest events of the foothill community, the annual Halloween bash.

We had just rented the video, Martin Scorsese's controversial epic, "The Last Temptation of Christ." I suggested we go to the party as Jesus and Mary Magdalene. Larry jumped at the idea.

We looked fantastic that night—not overdone and eerily realistic. Larry wore a long hair wig with a crown of thorns fashioned from dead branches. He found a muslin shirt, drawstring pants, and worn huarache sandals. I draped a blue and white striped muslin shawl over my long hair. I already had a muslin beach wrap that I wound around my waist with bike shorts underneath. A tasteful slit showed part of one leg.

I found a muslin gypsy top with flared sleeves that I tied up to show a patch of midriff. I wore many silver bracelets and necklaces, as well as anklets on my bare feet. We outlined our eyes with a dark kohl pencil for that ashy, haunted look. When we entered the party, groups of people broke apart to let us pass. Surreal. Immediately, Larry wandered off and mingled without me. I felt abandoned and vulnerable.

Larry called me later that week. "Why did you talk me into wearing those outrageous costumes?"

Where is this coming from?

Aghast, I responded. "What? You thought it was a great idea when I suggested it."

He seemed a bit angry. "Well, many people at the party were shocked. It was embarrassing."

Oh, come on, grow up.

"Funny," I said. "You seemed to be having the time of your life as the center of attention. You couldn't stop talking for days about being the hit of that party. Whatever discomfort you felt had nothing to do with me."

I felt like hitting a punching bag. "You know, Larry, you are giving me such mixed signals, I think it's best we go our separate ways. I don't think you are ready for any kind of relationship. I came out of a marriage of mixed signals. I don't have the strength or energy to go through that again."

"I guess you're right, Jeaninne. I'm sorry I made you feel uncomfortable. I really do like you."

We wished each other well.

I didn't see Larry again except to take him to the airport the following month when his ride canceled at the last minute. He had business in China. He pleaded with me to give him another chance on the way to the airport, promising to be less self-centered.

"I'll be gone a month, but when I get back after Christmas, we'll celebrate New Year's Eve together at all the major town parties. I'll keep in touch from China." I said I would think about it.

In the meantime, Chuck was not happy I was dating and tried desperately to get me back. In order to deal with all of these immature men, I booked a date to have professional photos taken with B.J. to put the focus back on her. She was the only thing that made sense in my life. We did the shoot under the aspen trees in front of my cabin. We wore red to match the last bastion of flaming autumn leaves still clinging to the trees. B.J.'s hair was beginning to grow out from her summer cut, which alleviated the possibility of ticks, fleas, and foxtails. I didn't care. I wanted to preserve our love in photos that would last a lifetime, with or without her luscious coat.

In the photo, I am squatting next to B.J. with my arms wrapped around her back and chest. We are cheek to cheek, looking straight into the camera. I look relaxed and happy; B.J. looks pensive and wise. My hands aren't relaxed. They grip into her body as if I never want to let her go. I look at this photo every single day to remind me that B.J. was my most enduring relationship up to that point in my life.

Larry called me once from China. The week he should have returned to the States, he didn't call me at all. A few days before the new year of 1990, I walked into the pub and saw him seated at the end of the bar.

"How was your trip, Larry?" He looked surprised to see me.

"Oh hi, Jeaninne! Hey listen, sorry I didn't call about our New Year's plans. I've been crazy busy." *Yeah, sitting at the bar drinking.*

"No problem. I didn't expect to hear from you." In fact, I had already met Rich, a young man ten years my junior. I knew Larry wouldn't take me anywhere for New Year's Eve.

"I bought you something in China. Maybe you could come by my house to pick it up." *That's not going to happen.*

"Or, you could bring it here." I wasn't about to go to his house and beg for a gift. (Larry dropped off a flower pattern vase on my porch a week after that conversation. I eventually auctioned it off at a charity event.)

At that exact moment, tall, dark, and handsome Rich, in all of his 6 foot 4 inch splendor, strode in from San Jose wearing a black leather motorcycle jacket and black leather pants.

All eyes turned on him. He crept up behind me and planted a kiss on my neck. I glanced at Larry and caught the wide-eyed look of incredulity on his face. In rare instances such as this one, the universe gifts us with impeccable timing.

Rich said, "Sorry I'm late, babe, I was stuck in Bay Area traffic." He looked so good in leather, I could have taken a bite out of him.

I couldn't resist the introduction. "Rich, this is Larry. He is also a Mad Dogs pub fan."

They shook hands, and then Rich grabbed me up from my stool and whisked me off to the dance floor. When we passed the full length of the bar, I looked over at Tony serving drinks. He witnessed the whole incident. He smiled and winked. I blew him a kiss.

Rich whispered in my ear, "Who was that guy you were talking to?"

I answered, "No one special. Just one of the locals."
Dignity. Check.

⌒

I was honored to have been part of the Nevada City
Theater's production of "Master Harold and the Boys," Athol
Fugard's controversial South African play written to bring
awareness to the theme of apartheid.

I enrolled in a Sierra College theater class during the spring
of 1991 to return to my theater passions. I needed an excuse
to break away from the seesawing emotions of my troubled
relationship with Chuck. I wasn't sure how to break away from
his influence. J.D., the director of "Master Harold" and also
my college instructor, recruited me to be a crew member in his
play—just what the doctor ordered.

I basked in my role as assistant stage manager, which
turned into a second job. I sneaked B.J. backstage for some
evening rehearsals. Because of her calm nature, no one even
noticed her. B.J. found a corner of the set to watch me scurry
around in panic mode. It was my job to keep the water pump
following against gravity—insuring the look and sound of
authentic rain outside of the set windows—setting out the
props, and keeping the actors on cue with entrances and exits.

Sometimes, B.J. padded up to the top tier where she slept soundly against the balcony wall, away from the hustle and bustle. I'd hear a cast or crew member from the house seats exclaim, "Oh, hi B.J. I didn't see you there."

From the wings, I witnessed a master class in every performance. The professional African American actors were on loan from the best acting institutions and academies in the country. I never tired of the same gut-wrenching scenes, night after night. Such raw emotion, always new and exciting, never sounded rehearsed.

I felt proud ushering the electrically charged actors on and offstage, making sure they hit their cues on time. None of the cast and crew could have predicted the controversy that erupted from "Master Harold and the Boys." I learned many deeper lessons on race during the run of that incredible play.

G.J., one of the lead actors, fascinated me. I fell hard for him during our backstage banter, even though he was ten years my junior. I figured anyone who possessed his intelligence and talent had to be amazing. Growing up in a multicultural, blue collar family, I never thought about race as something separate.

I grew up in the greater Los Angeles area; I dated men of all races before I met Ben. What kept me from falling in love with G.J. was our age difference. At twenty-six, he had his whole life ahead of him. At thirty-six, my maternal clock ticked loudly.

As the play progressed, word filtered out to the season ticket holders that "Master Harold" was a South African production performed by African American actors. Too busy herding actors and keeping the rain machine working, I didn't hear the buzz around town about race. B.J. and I kept focused on our work backstage, except for the much-needed fun we had with the crew and cast members.

However, ticket sales took a dive before opening night. Our director, J.D., encouraged us not to worry, he knew we were sitting on top of a hit. We filled the seats on opening night with friends and family members— standing room only! By the time we kicked off the season in May of 1991, the New York Times had already published an article on Nevada City's fleeing ticket holders. The story's hook—African Americans dared to perform in an all-white county. Appalled, I couldn't believe that a liberal, artistic town could be so ignorant and out of touch.

G.J. and I filled that summer with light-hearted fun before he had to resume his life at the San Francisco Conservatory Theater. We spent time on my turf in Nevada City with B.J. and time in Sacramento at his mid-town apartment with his

162

cat. G.J. showed me how African Americans deflected societal judgments in the form of prejudicial stares and negative comments. He showed me how people live in the face of dissent with their heads held high.

Once the news of "Master Harold" hit the papers, the theater filled up again—nothing but rave reviews for every performance. G.J. and the cast even visited the local schools for question and answer seminars about race in America, which was sorely overdue.

I still have our cast party pictures taken at J.D.'s house— two idealistic people with stars in their eyes, not possessing a clue of what might be soaring in the broad skies of their destinies.

Sadly, it would be a few years after that night in the pub with Rich when Tony, my British bartender friend and disc jockey colleague, lost his fight against Juvenile Diabetes.

The radio station, KVMR, gave him a lovely memorial in the foundry building. He left a sizeable hole in the hearts of those who knew him. A few years ago, when I was perusing Nevada City news online, I learned that Larry died from cancer in 2013. My silent prayers went out to his daughter who would be in her late thirties. I never heard from Rich again after I suggested that he return to his other love. I can't even remember his last name, but I hope he found his happily ever after.

I am thrilled to report that G.J. has carved out a fabulous life on Broadway, television, and movies, though I am hardly surprised. When I asked G.J. if he remembered B.J., he answered, "Of course, how can I forget that sweet girl?"

CHAPTER SEVENTEEN

ADVENTURERS

B.J. shared my peripatetic spirit. We carved out a life that satisfied our adventurous natures, but I also needed to be with family and lifelong friends at least four times a year. B.J. acted as my co-pilot from Grass Valley to Brea, California. We forged the eight-hundred-mile round-trip without air conditioning in my 1990 Rocky Daihatsu jeep. We left the mountains before dawn to arrive in Southern California by the afternoon, circumventing the brutal Central Valley heat. With many stops for water, walks, and nature calls, we made the trips in my tin can sports vehicle no worse for wear.

I spent my twenties wandering Europe, Canada, and Mexico whenever I had two cents to rub together. I attended higher education in the 1970's and 1980's when a young person could afford an apartment rental and a state college tuition with two jobs. I saved every cent for my summer sojourns, alone and with friends. Travel would always be in my blood. However, once B.J. came into my life, she was my first priority. It never occurred to me to travel without her.

Everyone who met B.J. fell under her spell. Hotels didn't turn her away, nor did boutique shop owners in places like Truckee, Carmel, and Laguna Beach allow her to stay tied up outside like a common backyard dog. B.J. exuded royalty and she knew it.

When I registered for my hotel rooms, B.J. sat outside of the glass doors in a sit-stay stance, staring in with the confidence of a queen presiding over her court. When I window-shopped in high-end boutiques, B.J. curled up in a ball to nap in the covered entryways, unobtrusive and unflappable.

"Whose beautiful dog is that?" Invariably, every shopkeeper asked that same question.

"Mine," I answered proudly. "Her name is B.J."

"Is she always this good?" Inevitably, the same question.

"Always." My unwavering answer.

"In that case, bring her in. She can hang out with us behind the desk."

Or, standard responses, in the case of most hotel clerks, occurred as follows:

"We don't allow pets in the rooms, but I can see how your well-behaved dog waits for you."

To which I replied, "Oh, she's fine locked in the car at night." I never left B.J. in the car because I sneaked her into my room after dark.

"Oh no, it's too cold for her to be in the car. You can take her in the room as long as you don't leave her unattended." That's when I winked down at my girl.

"Thank you so much. And believe me, she is never unattended."

Two incidents on my travels with B.J. remain indelibly carved in my memory. One is of a humorous nature, the other carved a deeper understanding of our love.

One of my stepfather's hard-earned possessions was his built-in swimming pool. My parents struggled to make ends meet for all of us, but an in-ground pool is almost a requirement in the desert heat of Southern California. Fred truly enjoyed having his children and grandchildren at the house for pool parties. Our large blended family defined him until his passing in November, 2016.

Whenever B.J. and I arrived hot and tired after a long drive, she ran through the house and made a beeline for the pool. My mother delighted in watching B.J. swim from one end of the pool to the other in her even, rhythmic strokes. We meditated on the perfection of her pace—paddle, glide, paddle, glide. One could set a watch to the seconds between each push.

My stepfather came home earlier than usual from a long, grueling day managing his Italian deli restaurant. He joined us outside as we watched B.J. swim. Mom shared her delight regarding B.J.'s water acuity.

"Fred, you have to watch B.J. swim. She keeps paddling from one end to the other, content as can be." Mom stood at the back slider pointing at B.J. gliding through the clear water.

"Marlene, I don't want that dog's hair clogging up the filter." Fred ducked back into the house to collapse in his TV room.

I guided B.J. out of the pool onto the warm cement. She sprawled out to dry her golden tresses. I'm sure that I heard slight breaths of pure pleasure as the sun caressed her body.

Mom wanted me to go shopping with her, so I asked Fred if we could leave B.J. in the grassy, shaded side yard with the pool gate latched. He agreed.

Upon our return, we heard Fred's voice coming from the backyard.

"Go on, girl. Dive in. It's okay." B.J. sat next to the pool steps at perfect attention, staring attentively into my stepfather's face. She respected the rules.

Mom raised an index finger to her lips so that I wouldn't say anything. We stood silently at the sliding doors and watched as Fred encouraged B.J. to dive into the pool. When Fred saw us, he looked up sheepishly and said, "Jeaninne, tell B.J. she can go in the pool."

B.J. tentatively entered the pool via the steps, not sure if the snarly man was truly serious. Once submerged, she cut through the water like a playful dolphin, fully present in the rhythm of her strokes. Fred stood at the edge of the pool, hands on his hips, an imperceptible smile fighting to break free. My mother, nor I, said a word.

The second memorable trip experience with B.J. gave me new insight into the soul of my golden girl, one I could have never imagined. Ricky, who was with me when I met Ben, lived in Topanga Canyon above Malibu in a sprawling ranch house. Situated at the end of a mountain wall, only one road led to and from her house.

Locals allowed their dogs to run freely in packs. I had no idea that these dogs would become a cause for concern until B.J. and I waited in Ricky's car port one late August afternoon.

We arrived at her home after eight hours of driving. Ricky told me she might be late coming back from an appointment in Los Angeles, so I unfolded my yoga mat on her cement car port. With my hand weights, I ran through my floor work to stretch and ease tight muscles from the long drive. B.J. relaxed beside me.

A pack of large dogs approached us in a careful manner, wondering about the new canine that had invaded their territory. They stayed on the asphalt driveway, but spread out around us in a semi-circle. B.J. stood up and placed her body in front of mine. I stretched my neck to see above all 80 pounds of her. I didn't stand up suddenly for fear of frightening the curious dogs.

A shepherd mix inched towards B.J. The other canines of various mixed breeds followed the shepherd's lead. I witnessed a side of my girl that had never been tested before this day.

B.J. growled from the depth of her belly, erupting into one fierce howl. The hair on her back stood up. Pearl white incisors, sharp and menacing, flashed out of her snarling muzzle. B.J. had returned to her ancient instincts. She was no longer a coddled housepet, she was a wolf mother, ready to die protecting one of her own.

The alpha dog made an abrupt turn, taking the other dogs with him. I held my breath until they trotted down the steep driveway and disappeared into the canyon below. Shaking, I grabbed B.J. and hugged her tightly. A swell of love and gratitude for this amazing creature, who proved she would have fought to the death for me, filled the core of my being. B.J. made me a better person.

As Ricky drove up the driveway, B.J. broke away from my embrace and greeted her old friend with a stick one of the pack dogs had dropped in haste.

CHAPTER EIGHTEEN

JACK

My biological father, Jack, never met B.J. Our father-daughter relationship was almost non-existent. My charismatic father, proud of how I had conducted my independent life without any financial compensation, didn't believe in helping his children financially, even when he had the means. My father and mother married fresh out of high school. The dawn of the 1950's, when every young married couple wanted a few children, a new car in the garage and the white picket fence, defined a generation. We post-war children, the Baby Boomers, exploded onto the scene filling neonatal hospital units to capacity across America. My brother, Steven, appeared in 1951. I made my debut in 1954.

Ironically, I take after my father in looks and personality; however, our politics and values were at opposite ends of the spectrum. I inherited my compassion and kindness from my mother. Jack was solely about succeeding in the corporate world of sales and being the life of any party.

My father knew how to work a room. Every person in my father's circle was drawn to his charming ways. For example, he could tell a joke better than anyone I ever knew. He entertained his colleagues with funny antidotes about work, while flirting with their wives.

At five-feet, ten inches, Jack seemed much taller. His broad shoulders, long torso, and narrow hips made his legs look longer. My mother said he reminded her of the actor, Tony Curtis; but to me, Jack was more exotic, like the actor, Tyrone Power. His black curly hair, cut short to his head, framed his almond-shaped green eyes.

Jack's wide smile reflected two rows of perfectly straight, pearly white teeth. No one could dispute my father's quarter Pechanga Indian bloodlines when it came to his prominent nose and olive skin.

However, as a political conservative, he was ashamed of his indigenous heritage and only identified with his French ancestry.

After Jack left my mother in 1963, my brother and I saw him every other weekend for a few years. Those weekends consisted of watching TV in a smoke-filled family room while he and his wife sipped on the cocktails of the day—vodka, whiskey, bourbon.

My new stepmother's oldest daughter, six years my senior, moved out at seventeen. Her youngest daughter, three years my junior, was usually with her father when we visited. It didn't occur to my father to take us camping, to the beach, or to an amusement park for child-centered fun like he did when we were a family. As long as we stayed one weekend night twice a month, he was fulfilling the court order.

Jack did take us to the movies in opulent old theaters in downtown L.A., but only to watch mature, R-rated movies he and his wife preferred. We were required to adapt to their weekend activities, not the other way around.

By the time we were well into our teens, we opted to cut our visits to every Christmas Day and maybe a few times during the summer. That was pretty much the extent of my relationship with my father.

My brother, Steve, entered the music business where his work as an engineer kept him from visiting our father during his young adulthood. My father made it clear years before, he didn't time for my brother's angst or adolescent forays into drugs and alcohol. Ironically, it was the loss of their father/son relationship that caused my brother's descent into decades of substance abuse before he finally found his sobriety.

As I matured, I enjoyed grown-up conversations with Jack about how he navigated the business world. One bit of advice that came from my father's business acumen makes perfect sense for the corporate world—if you have a good marketing idea, propose it in a way that makes your boss think he or she thought of it. That is one of the reasons my father advanced so quickly.

I am thankful for two special times in my formative years that I experienced with my father, just the two of us. Those events helped me to understand him better in my adult years.

As an eighth grader in the 1967-68 school year, Jack asked me to join him for the most popular college football game of the fall season—the infamous rivalry between USC and UCLA. My father was like a kid on Christmas morning as we walked from the parking lot of the Los Angeles Coliseum into the stadium on that sunny autumn day.

Settling into our nose-bleed seats high above the field, Jack announced, "You have to have a stadium hot dog smothered in mustard and relish. It isn't football without a few dogs and a double bag of peanuts." I salivated because I could taste the food he described.

At the concession stand, Dad jockeyed his food and a red plastic cup brimming with beer while I concentrated on not spilling my large soda, peanut bag, and super-sized hot dog.

I felt the anticipation of this much-publicized event as crisply as the dying leaves on the Maple trees that outlined the arena.

Captivated in the late afternoon sun, I listened to my father's thoughts about the finer points of football while mustard dripped on my blue and white plaid tennis shoes. For those few hours, I was Jack's only audience.

I savored every moment sharing binoculars next to my radiant father. My senses sparked with the booming of the USC marching band, the muscular white horse carrying a red-caped Trojan warrior, exuberant cheerleaders somersaulting in the air, the colorful student posters flipped to spell out chants, and USC golden boy, O.J. Simpson, running onto the field. When the crowd erupted into a collective roar, I anticipated the action ahead.

Two hours after cheering with America's youth, we exited the stadium with those same students pushing and shoving in a race to the parking lot. I don't even remember who won. I grabbed onto my father's arm because this was the closest we had ever been since he left.

"Oh, Sweetheart, don't do that, I don't want people to think I'm a dirty old man." Jack looked to his right and left, self-conscious of his appearance with his pre-teen daughter.

"But dad, I'm only thirteen, and I look just like you." I felt dirty and discarded.

"Yes, but you look older." *Who cares? I'm your daughter.*

I let go of Jack's arm and tucked the memories of that football game into the recesses of my mind. The magic had disappeared by the time I clicked my seat belt.

⌒

At seventeen, in the summer of 1971, Jack asked me to stay with him and work in his office for a week. Farmer Brothers Coffee was expanding, moving from downtown Los Angeles to Long Beach. I was thrilled to have more time with my father, away from the wife who never warmed to us.

The first morning of that week, my long sun-kissed hair and bronze tan glistened in my pink scooped neck, A-line mini dress. We stopped at L.A.'s famous Randy's Donuts, home of the giant statue donut, to take dozens back to his office staff. I enjoyed passing out the variety of bakery delights to Jack's employees who found my father irresistible. The work was repetitive, yet comforting.

I felt important filing, answering phones, and organizing paperwork in boxes marked for the move.

I welcomed the opportunity to add extra college money to a job I had for two years at a high-end dress boutique in La Habra Fashion Square. I cherished the feeling that my father seemed proud of me.

"Mr. Farmer, meet my daughter, Jeaninne. She will be helping us organize for the move. Yes, she is pretty; but more important, she is extremely bright. I am proud of her work ethic and all that she has accomplished in just three years of high school." *Maybe Dad did love me.*

"Nice to meet you, sir. My father has spoken highly of you. Thank you for allowing me this opportunity." I looked over at my father to see the pride in his face.

Driving home that day, my father said, "Yes, daughter, you are definitely a chip off the old block. You made my boss feel special today, and that's how you work your way up the corporate ladder.

I can't believe you want to be a teacher. Why work for the government when you can make money in the private sector world of profit?"

"I don't want to be rich, Dad. I want to make a difference in children's lives." *Well, his pride for my work was good while it lasted.*

"Oh Honey, that's all good and noble, but what quality of life will you have?" *My father honestly doesn't get me.*

"The quality of life I want."

Jack didn't give me away when I married Ben. He showed up for the ceremony, preferring not to participate in the pomp and circumstance of a wedding that centered around my stepfather's family.

The last picture of me taken with my father was at my wedding on April 15th, 1983. We both look stiff, our identical smiles a bit forced. Yet, I cherish that photo.

The only time I asked for financial help from my father was for a fifty-dollar text book in my senior year of college. My waitress job at a five-star restaurant covered all my expenses, but I couldn't pay for the book until my next paycheck.

"Hi Dad. Listen, I was wondering if you could spot me fifty dollars for a text book. I can pay you back next week when I get paid. I have to have it by Monday, it's for a 4 unit lab class."

"I am sick and tired of you kids asking me for car loans and back rent. You know, Jeaninne, I wish I could have gone to college." I could tell he had been drinking.

"Dad, I have never asked you for anything. Ever. I have paid for every cent of my college, without any help from you or Mom. You know I will pay you back. That was your choice to get married after high school. You could have gone to college at any time." That last parting comment was my anger getting the best of me.

"Sorry, Sweetheart, you are on your own." His words slurred together.

"Haven't I always been on my own? Never mind, Dad."

Click.

I was able to get an emergency loan from the university the next day, which I paid back the following week.

I was surprised when my dad gave us five hundred dollars for our wedding. Ben and I foolishly spent it on winter ski gear.

Jack and Ben never developed a father-son relationship. We saw my father only a few times during the Christmas holidays throughout our four years together. Like my marriage, my relationship with my father was meant for a limited shelf life.

I talked about B.J. over the years with my father, but I didn't bring her for visits. I didn't want her left on their pristine patio, nor exposed to a smoke-filled den where Jack liked to watch endless football games and golf tournaments.

We left B.J. at my mother's house where she was truly loved and appreciated. Nothing about my father's life was conducive to children or pets. If he couldn't be near a cigarette, a drink, or a groomed golf course, he was like a fish out of water. B.J. represented everything Jack was not.

My father called me once after Ben left to offer his condolences. I remember an awkward conversation with few words of comfort, but I appreciated Dad's sobriety.

My stepfather, who was also uncomfortable with emotional conversations, connected with me on a more compassionate level. I felt that Fred actually listened to me and gave me the time to vent. Jack didn't know how to string his words into sentences of comfort, ending our call after a few light-hearted minutes of banter about his golf game.

I appreciated my father's guarded concern and reassured him that I would be fine. We resumed our Christmas visits whenever I was in Southern California.

However, for most of the late 1980's, Jack and his wife stayed in Las Vegas during the holidays. Our relationship whittled down to a few phone calls a year until February 1st, 1990.

"Hello, Jeaninne. I hope this is the right number. This is Patty, your father's neighbor. I'm sorry to report that your father passed away today. He was driving home from work when he had a massive heart attack. You can call his wife for more information. Again, I'm so sorry. We loved Jack and will miss his presence in our lives."

I stared at my answering machine for several minutes before I played the message over and over. Emotionally paralyzed, B.J. and Boogers gathered around me, sensing their mom's shock. The first thought I clearly remember: *And of course, his wife had a stranger break the news.*

"Chuck, it's me. My father died today. Can you come up? I don't know what to do. Do I call his wife, my mother, my brother, all of the above?" *Why did I call Chuck first?*

"Oh, Jeaninne, I'm so sorry. I can't come up because I'm cooking dinner for my children, it's rare that all of our schedules mesh. Why don't you join us? Bring B.J. and spend the night."

Too distraught to realize the insanity of driving down the mountain to be in the middle of a family celebration, I should have grieved at home privately. I called my mother who advised me to fly home immediately, but I couldn't think straight to make sudden arrangements for my job and my girls.

I numbly packed up an overnight bag and drove B.J. down the mountain before the light of day took its leave for the night.

Chuck and his three teenagers were in the middle of a festive family meal when I walked into his mobile home. He seated me at the end of the long, dark wood antique table as if I were the guest of honor at some joyful celebration.

I felt like a cardboard cut-out—emotionally flat, depleted, sad. I assumed that Chuck's children knew about my father because of the way their eyes darted away from mine. No one said anything to me. *What am I doing here?* I was that crazy relative no one wanted to acknowledge.

After a pretend bite of food, I couldn't control my grief. I called for B.J., who was curled up in front of the pot belly stove in the corner of the living room, and then excused myself from the table. She followed me out to the pasture land.

Under the moonlight, I sobbed into B.J.'s back, clinging on to her in desperation.

"Oh, B.J., I can't believe my father's gone. What do I do now?" And then I looked down at my patient girl and felt a stabbing lightning bolt of relief. B.J. was still by my side, loving, loyal, true. I said something to her out loud that has stuck with me ever since.

"I feel bad for my father, and for the relationship we will never have, B.J., but if I lost you, I couldn't cope. Your love means more because you have always loved me back, without question. Just like Mom, you would die for me. Because we have each other, Sweet Girl, everything will be okay. Mommy loves you so very much." B.J. licked my face until the tears were gone.

We walked the land for an hour so that I could catch my breath. "Come on girl, let's go home." I put B.J. in my car, sneaked into the mobile and grabbed my bag in the entryway. No one heard me. I drove home with a broken heart.

My brother and I stayed for a few days at our mother's house for the memorial service held in Huntington Beach. I left B.J. with my classroom aide and her family. Her teenaged boys spoiled B.J. on their ranch, not far from Chuck's property. I decided to ease out of Chuck's life the night of my father's death. When I ran out of the trailer that night during dinner, Chuck didn't leave the table to find me. He called when he realized my car was gone.

"I should have canceled my dinner and drove up to comfort you instead of allowing you to drive so far in your state of grief. Sometimes, I just don't think." Chuck clearly wanted my forgiveness.

I no longer cared. "And I was a fool for driving down. I get it. Your children come first, as they should. However, all I wanted from you was a warm hug during an exceptionally hard time." Chuck's voice softened. "I am sorry about your father, Jeaninne." I felt too betrayed to respond. Another father figure turned his back on me.

The officiant delivered a surreal service for my father. He clearly belonged to the funeral home as he knew nothing about Jack nor his family. He pontificated words of honor and respect for a man who lived a selfish life.

It had been years since I had seen Jack's stepdaughters or friends from his past. My brother and I stood in front of his open casket, clinging on to each other. Jack's once handsome body had decayed into a withered shell doused in thick pancake make-up. I vowed at the sight of him to prevent my loved ones from being put on display after death. Our souls are what matter, not the useless casings we leave behind.

Jack's wife didn't give us any of our father's personal items and she made sure we didn't receive one penny of his inheritance. The older stepsister sneaked out a framed picture collage I made for Jack as a Christmas present when I was in college. She gave it to me when we drove back up to Northern California together after the funeral.

I cherish those photos I had carefully chosen of our happier times—that same collage sat neglected in the back of Jack's closet for years.

Twenty years passed before the younger stepsister sent me my father's childhood photo albums. I'm grateful to have them now. I've since found two heartfelt letters in attic boxes that Jack wrote to me at different times in my life, the only remnants left of our connection.

With the passage of time, I have gained the wisdom that my father loved us in the only shallow way he knew how.

CHAPTER NINETEEN

GETAWAYS

L ife resumed with B.J. and Boogers on the ranch, but loneliness seeped through me like a wet fog. I dated without truly letting go of Chuck. In my single life full of fleeting, questionable delights, he remained my comfort food, safe and predictable. I even succumbed to two trips with Chuck before I pulled the plug for good.

Chuck enticed me with a trip to Hawaii. Another teacher friend and his wife were able to secure a good deal on tickets so I could afford my share. Chuck wanted them to accompany us to make a fun foursome. After my father's death, I needed an escape. We booked a time share on the island of Kauai for one week. Joan, my classroom aide, and her teen boys were always happy to watch sweet B.J. Boogers preferred to stay at home with Laura and Tybo. I cleared the decks for what I imagined would be a renewal of spirit as I forged ahead with my new identity as a fatherless child.

Chuck and I bickered in the car until we reached the airport. As he had the night of my father's death, he treated me with indifference, his default way of distancing himself. I didn't succumb. Determined to enjoy my vacation, I put my sorrow on hold, with or without him.

"Well, there are no seats together on this flight. We can give up our seats for another flight tomorrow with the added bonus of a free flight voucher. I can take my daughter on a trip and you can take your mother somewhere nice, Jeaninne." Chuck seemed excited about skipping the flight, not concerned at all about what I wanted. *Why do I expect him to be any different?*

I snapped back, "Chuck, you can wait for the next flight tomorrow, I'm getting on this plane now." Chuck looked like he woke up from a screeching alarm. He finally looked at me.

The other couple also wanted to leave right away, so Chuck relented. We didn't sit together, which was a relief. I needed to regain my composure by returning to my books and my music tapes.

The refreshing breezes off the Kauai shoreline beckoned me to drop my bags on the bed, jump into my running shorts, and run on the sand until I dropped from exhaustion. The emotions I had buried for my father welled up and exploded into messy, ugly sobs.

Again, I fled from Chuck, wondering why I had agreed to travel with him, as I had thoughtlessly agreed to drive to his ranch the night my father died. With my emotions released, I ran back to the others and joined them on the beach front patio for that much needed tropical drink, topped with fresh fruit and a little paper umbrella.

I swallowed my pride, allowing myself a relaxing vacation on the alluring garden island. I accepted that Chuck and I were done as a couple; yet, our friendship wasn't hindered from experiencing a great time with good people.

When I look back on our photos, I see sumptuous seafood meals, pristine beaches bereft of trash, challenging hikes on mossy cliffs above crashing seas, silly tennis matches on the hotel grounds, golf games on courses with panoramic views of the ocean, and much laughter. Chuck made me laugh. Laughter is completely underrated as a cure for whatever ails.

Snorkeling a few hundred feet from our beach cove, just past the breakers, I glimpsed at a small tiger shark swimming below me. I screamed, "Shark!" Chuck thought I saw a Great White the way I swam back to shore like a cartoon character whose arms had become helicopter blades. He laughed so hard, he almost choked on the crashing waves.

We spent one day hiking up and down scenic switchback trails. I snapped picture after picture. When we returned to the room to nap before for a nice dinner, I looked in my camera to grab out the finished roll. Nothing. No roll. More laughter.

That night at dinner, Chuck got hit with a horrible case of island revenge. He spent most of the evening in the restaurant's elegant bathroom exclaiming, "It's gorgeous in here!" We left the island as friends.

I returned home with a new perspective. Once B.J. was back in my arms, it hit me, "You are open and ready for change, Jeaninne. It can only get better from this moment forward."

Chuck approached me later that summer with a proposition. "My sister and her husband offered to sell their week in a time share cabin on South Lake Tahoe. Would you like to bring B.J. before school starts? I've invited my children and my best friend from Southern California. My sister and her husband want to see you, as well."

That seems harmless enough. With friends and family, there would be no room for complicated expectations between us.

"Okay," I said. "That might be kind of fun. B.J. loves Tahoe."

The week started off in a flurry of festivities. Chuck's children, ages 15, 17, and 19, showed up with their friends on the first day. We spent the day on the lake watching happy teens diving and flipping off of the dock, goofing on each other the way healthy teenagers do.

Chuck was in his element, surrounded by his attractive, creatively intelligent children who always made him proud. B.J. was lavished with enthusiastic, adolescent attention. I enjoyed reading my books and magazines to the background sounds of unabashed youth.

I felt like a close friend of the Kennedys when I was around Chuck's cultured family. Like the Kennedys, in Chuck's clan, intelligent discussions flourished around the dining table; education was everything.

Chuck's sister and her husband also taught in public schools. Proud of my activist role in education, I connected with their liberal values and emphasis on community service. I strove for excellence to be worthy of being a peer among such passionate and brilliant people.

However, I didn't realize that Chuck's kids and their friends would be staying the entire week in the large loft room upstairs. What I thought was going to be family time during the day, with quiet time in the evenings for adults, became more of an adolescent summer camp. I had become a camp counselor, cleaning up messes and cooking with Chuck. It would have been fun if Chuck and I were still in a relationship; instead, I felt like hired help.

I slowly disappeared into the background of all the commotion. B.J. and I ran around the lake for hours each day, stealing swims along the way. I wallowed in the tranquility of being surrounded by the imposing Sierra Mountains and the iridescent blue green waters of Lake Tahoe.

An overwhelming sense of loneliness prompted me to call Ben from a pay phone at a gas station mini-mart. Halfway back to the cabin during one of our five-mile daily lake runs, I weakened in a moment of vulnerability.

"Hello, Ben. It's Jeaninne." My body shook.

"Jeaninne! How are you?" Ben sounded pleasant.

"My father died."

Pause.

"Oh, I'm so sorry. Are you alright?"

He seemed genuinely concerned.

"Yeah, even though we weren't close, he was my father. He had a massive heart attack in traffic. You know, Jack often said, 'I want to die young with a good-looking corpse.' Well, he got half his wish, he died young. Sorry, when I'm nervous, I revert to dark humor."

"I understand. How's B.J.?" I detected a bit of sadness.

"She's always great. She's curled up at my feet right now. I couldn't have survived our divorce and my dad's death without her. Thank you for leaving B.J. with me."

"I wouldn't have thought to take her away from you. B.J. was always your dog."

"So, how are you, Ben? Do you still love jumping out of planes into fires?"

"Yes. The best decision I ever made. Thank you for encouraging me to realize this life-long dream."

I'm so relieved I left you with something positive.

"Listen, Ben. I really wanted to apologize for not being the wife you deserved. I need to stop beating myself up about it and ask for your forgiveness. You are a good man."

My body stopped shaking.

"No, Jeaninne. I need to ask for *your* forgiveness. I wasn't even close to being the man you deserved. If I could take back all the needless anger and jealousy, I would. I do hope you're happy." *Thank you, Ben, I actually believe you.*

"Well, I wouldn't go so far as to say happy, but I'm getting stronger. I am grateful for my life as a teacher and sharing it with B.J. Are you seeing anyone?"

I can't believe I asked him that.

Pause.

"Yes. I'm engaged." I didn't expect to feel a physical gut punch.

"Wow! Congrats. Do I know her?" I didn't want Ben to feel my sorrow.

"You met her parents when we drove through Colorado on one of our trips to Southern California. She is a friend of the family I lived with in high school when I couldn't stand being in Chicago. We share the same interests and she knows my family history."

"I'm truly happy for you, Ben. You deserve the right woman. Well, listen, I'm running out of coins. Thank you for this closure. I can move on knowing that you're in a good place." I did need this closure.

"Again, I'm sorry about your father, Jeaninne. Give the Beej a big hug for me."

"I will."

Hug B.J.—the only thing that sustained me each day.

Click.

My knees buckled. I collapsed to the curb, wrapping my arms around my golden girl and burying my tears into that dependable soft, silky coat.

"Okay, girl, I'm done. Let's go." My feet felt as though they had been encased in cement buckets.

B.J. picked up her leash, the one Ben had made especially for her out of horse lead rope. Staring squarely into my eyes, the red rope hung from each side of her droopy lip flaps. B.J.'s eyes stayed locked on me when she dropped it at my feet. She willed me to get up.

"You are absolutely right, B.J. I need to brush myself off and put one foot in front of the other. No more looking back." With B.J. in the lead, we ran back to the cabin watching the sun slip behind the horizon.

CHAPTER TWENTY

*H*EALING

Chuck graciously paid me back for my half of the Lake Tahoe cabin, he bought my plane ticket to visit my brother in Arizona. He agreed that the week in Lake Tahoe was more for his family than the relaxing vacation he had promised for us. Chuck was a friend, first and foremost.

The school year of 1990-91 started off without a hitch. I threw myself into my teaching, delivered my teen talk radio show each week, and signed up for acting classes at the community college. Being busy kept the loneliness at bay. I was so used to touching bases with Chuck at work, I became concerned when he failed to show up for a few days in a row. I called his sister to get answers.

"Hi Julie, Chuck hasn't been at work and I'm worried. It's not like him."

"Yes, I know. Thank you for calling. His depression has spiraled, so I'm going to keep him with me starting tomorrow." I knew it.

"Is there anything I can do?"

"I hate to impose, but could you come by and be with him tonight? We have previous plans and I don't want to leave him alone in that cold trailer."

"I can do better than that. I can take him up to Chicago Park to stay with me for one night." No one should stay in his mobile home without heat.

B.J. and I escorted our frail friend into my car from the rickety steps of his dilapidated mobile home. I looked out upon his 200 acres of untamed land, which included a running creek and a shallow lake. I thought about all the stories Chuck told about raising his children on this property handed down from generations: their brown bodies swinging from tree ropes into a large creek pool; camping in teepees by the lake's edge; chasing the cows that were leased to graze the vast pasture land; open pit barbecues and sleeping under the stars along the ever-flowing Coon Creek.

I could see this vibrant man in the middle of all this action, teaching his brood to fish, swinging out on the tree rope with three children clinging to every part of him. It pained me to see the virile man I held up looking so feeble. He tripped down three small steps.

Chuck had lost thirty pounds. Despondent, he lamented about not being a worthy father. Absolutely not true. I witnessed how much his children were his reason to exist, he lived for them. Chuck gave up his own comforts to send his children to the best universities. Bipolar Disorder is a thief. It robs a person's dignity and stomps it into the ground.

B.J. rested her head on Chuck's shoulder, suspecting something was not right. He reached back and stroked her broad, open face. "Oh, B.J., you are such a sweetheart." Her compassion and wisdom to know when her humans needed her never ceased to amaze me.

I expected that Friday night to be a long one in my little cabin on Dr. Laura's horse ranch. After I fixed Chuck his favorite tacos with chili beans and all the fixings, we watched a bit of TV.

Chuck insisted on staying in the living room on my large velvet couch to write urgent thoughts in his journal—the sleep switch in his brain was stuck on the off position. Bipolar

Disorder messes with the brain's electrical circuitry like an obsolete video tape jammed in an old VCR.

B.J. plopped down on the floor next to Chuck. When I called her to bed, she averted her attention away from my gaze, looking back at Chuck. I received her message loud and clear, *No, Mom, I'm needed here.*

B.J. was on a mission to watch over the manic man next to her—the man who could not stop his tormented thoughts from kidnapping his soul. I fell into bed without removing my clothes. Exhaustion had won.

B.J. nudged me out of sleep the next morning to follow her into the living room. Chuck, curled up in a ball, cried from somewhere deep and unreachable.

His notebooks spread out over the floor. I picked one up and could not make any sense of it. A jumble of illegible scribblings, proof of a mind wandering in a chaotic maze with no way out.

"I'll fix you some eggs, fruit and toast, Chuck, and then we'll go for a walk. You need fresh air." I needed to keep busy.

Chuck resisted, but with B.J.'s help, we got him out the door. He protested the whole mile down the forested highway to the Chicago Park Store.

"Please let me go back, I can't do this. I'm not worthy. Let me disappear, I'm not good for anyone. Why do you bother?"

Chuck wore a gray sweatshirt and jeans too big for his shrinking body. He shuffled along the road in worn tennis shoes like a hospital patient holding on to a hydration drip rack. I acted as the rack; B.J. kept the pace in the lead. Even his shaggy hair couldn't be tamed.

I responded, "This is not you talking, Chuck. It's a chemical imbalance. You are deprived of sleep, food, and energy. You can rest after this walk. The fresh air and adrenaline will help put your electrolytes back in balance." I made it all up, but it seemed logical.

B.J. maintained a few steps ahead of Chuck on her long leash, encouraging us to follow her pace. I held on to his elbow to make sure he didn't turn back. It took twice as long to get home, but we did it, one slow, tortuous step at a time.

Some moments fall between the brain's synaptic bridges rendering them lost. That day jumped over the gaps between the synaptic connections of my brain and stuck the landing in my memory bank. I can easily retrieve those images of Chuck walking tentatively between B.J. and me as clearly as snapshots pasted in a photo album. With her head jutting forward and her long determined steps pulling on the leash, she led us on that two-mile walk with the confidence of an intrepid explorer. Chuck allowed B.J. to lay in his lap in front of the TV until I drove him back to his sister's that evening. His confusion remained, but he appeared a little less tormented.

Chuck regained his mental equilibrium with medication and the support of family and friends. My future waited patiently. The years between 1990 and 1993 were hopeful and productive. I concentrated on new heights in my career as a grant writer and mentor teacher for the district. I also enjoyed helping Dr. Laura with her ranch menagerie.

I bottle-fed baby goats and baby raccoons; I sheared Jimmy Dean's hog fangs in the barn after Laura sedated the angry beast; and, I babysat Tybo whenever she left town for a few days. I concentrated on letting my emotional wounds heal with the beings I loved the most, B.J. and Boogers.

"Jeaninne, it's Julie."

"Oh, so nice to hear from you, Julie." Chuck's sister never called me, so I was worried something had happened to Chuck one Saturday morning in late June, 1993.

"Listen, I had a brainstorm this morning. Our grandfather's Victorian home is going to be up for rent in a month. I thought of you first. I know you love your adorable cabin in the woods, but this would be an opportunity to be blocks from the middle school in the center of Old Town Lincoln. You are pretty secluded up there in the Grass Valley foothills with so far to drive."

"You're right, Julie, I do often complain about my fear of being trapped at the end of this dead-end road in case of a forest fire." Ben taught me how flammable Manzanita bushes can be so close to a structure. Laura liked the way they looked.

"Wow, let me think about it, Julie, and I'll get back to you soon." *Could this be the sign I've needed to move my life closer to my job and the wider world, in general?*

I sat for a few minutes in silence weighing the possibilities of another move. B.J. pushed open the front door I left ajar. She liked to come and go while I cleaned on Saturday mornings. She placed a paw on my knee, her way of asking why I seemed so lost in thought.

"What do you think, Beej? Should we move again? I could save money on gas and it would be nice to regain the two hours of wasted commute time each day, not to mention saving wear and tear on the car. We would also be within walking distance of our school and the downtown shops. Julie's rent is exceptionally reasonable for such a spacious home.

I could even save money for a home of our own. I know you would miss Laura and Tybo, as would I, but we have so many friends in Lincoln. This has been a wonderful place to start over after Ben left, but change can be good, right?"

B.J. cocked her head, seeming to sense this possible change of direction. Sensing the energy shift in the room, my loyal old Siamese cat, Boogers, joined us on the yellow plastic couch.

I wrapped my arms around my girls and said, "Why not? Let's do it!"

CHAPTER TWENTY-ONE

MEMORIES

Thrilled she would no longer have to worry about me living in isolation with that long drive through inclement weather, my mother's relief became mine. Chuck offered to help me move, as he had when we left the Nursery Street house in Nevada City. I dreaded breaking the news to Laura and her beloved pooch, Tybo. My emotions jumped all over the map. I spent days walking the ranch, memorizing every inch of it.

"Oh Tybo, we will miss your spikey bangs, gray beard, and those perky, expressive ears. Won't we B.J.?" I cupped Tybo's face in my hands while B.J. sat close to him. He wagged his stump as if I had promised him the finest T-bone steak. I laughed remembering how he stole B.J.'s sticks and then enticed her to steal them back. Or, the time we came home in a torrential rain storm to find Tybo sopping wet, shivering on our porch. I was his person when Laura worked late. I brought him in and towel-dried him by the wall furnace. He and B.J. flanked me in cuddles while I read all evening.

B.J. and I enjoyed our last runs down the gravel road that spilled onto Highway 174 between Chicago Park and Grass Valley. The ever-present German Shepherds, loose in the yard of their gun-toting owner, no longer charged at us from their bivouac of brittle bushes.

I learned by trial and error to soothe them with baby talk. B.J. submissively rolled over on her back when we passed by their dark, dilapidated house tucked back from the road. We became part of the pack soon after we moved to Dr. Laura's ranch.

I thought of how Laura had become a guardian angel to all of us, B.J., Boogers, and me. In those ranch years between 1989 and 1993, I applied to be a Big Sister in the Big Brother/ Big Sister program.

Already in my late thirties, I worried about not ever having a family of my own, so I decided to test run parenthood before considering single-parent adoption. I matched with a preteen girl whose single mother didn't have time for her daughter's extra-curricular pursuits.

This aloof girl was a tom-boy who loved sports and video games. I didn't care for team sports or video games; I was that quintessential girly girl. But this girl, Becky, agreed to give me a chance once she met B.J. She mentioned she enjoyed roller blading around the streets of Grass Valley. I figured I could give this activity my best Girl Scout effort. From the outset, I thought someone dropped the ball matching Becky with me.

After several days of skating on roller blades around the flat sidewalks of the middle school, I strapped on those blades to practice in my own neighborhood. I felt confident and ready for the challenge of the foothills close to home to fulfill my Big Sister role.

"B.J., are you ready to run with me while I skate?" B.J. ran to the car and hopped in, recognizing the familiar skates I placed next to her in the backseat. She had grown accustomed to my roller blade laps around our school playground.

I had scouted out a new medical facility a few miles down Highway 174. It appeared to have level sidewalks, perfect for a novice inline skater. I put on knee and arm pads, but foolishly neglected to buy a helmet. With B.J. jogging beside me, I started off strong, pushing one foot off at a time—push roll, push roll. "B.J., now we can skate up here after school."

She looked up at me grinning with delight to be on this new adventure in our neck of the woods.

Too confident in my limited experience on those slippery blades, I picked up speed. B.J. skidded to a halt. I looked back at her before I saw the sudden descent looming in front of me. The flat sidewalk had become a 45-degree drop down a long winding hill to the freeway below. I never practiced how to hockey stop on cement. I simply rolled onto the grass when I wanted to stop.

After I screamed bloody murder for several feet, going *at least* twenty miles per hour straight down the hill, I dropped onto the sidewalk using my butt as a brake. My head bounced off the pavement before I rolled into the dirt. B.J. galloped to my side in full panic mode. She panted and shook so hard, I thought she might collapse. I jumped up to assure B.J. that I would be fine. She licked the scrapes on my hands and legs with the sole purpose of healing my bloody wounds.

"Come on, girl, let's walk back up to the car." B.J. followed, plastered to my side.

A pregnant woman driving a van pulled over. She had seen the whole debacle from the ridge of the medical building parking lot. In my post-shock haze, I thought, *Wow, a woman in her condition stopping to help me. How sweet.*

"Excuse me, Miss. I think you need medical attention. Have you seen your backside?"

I looked back to what can only be described as raw hamburger meat. Both of my butt cheeks had lost the top layer of skin. My shorts were bloody and torn to shreds. *Oh Lord, I hope I don't lose my lunch in front of this nice woman.*

"Jump in. I'll take you and your gorgeous dog back up to the clinic. Here, sit on this towel." It hurt to sit, but I had no choice. I most likely would have fainted from shock if I had to walk back up that steep hill. I thanked this woman profusely who drove by just when I needed her. B.J. laid her head in my lap. *My loyal girl, what would I do without you?*

The doctor disinfected my bottom, meticulously extracting gravel bits with sharp steel tongs. He clicked his teeth and said, "Wow, there's no end to these incessant little rocks." Not the least bit comforting. Upon bandaging the open wounds, the doctor advised me to have someone check on my thought processes for the next 24 hours in case of a concussion.

"You shouldn't be driving back home. Is there someone you can call?" I thought of Chuck, but didn't want to waste precious time listening to his excuses about why he couldn't commit to the long drive into the foothills.

I feigned my concern and said, "It's okay, I have my dog tied up outside in the foyer, and I need to get her home. We only live a couple miles up the road. My neighbor, a doctor, will check on me. Other than the pain in my butt, I feel fine." He shook his head and smiled at my feeble attempt at humor.

The doctor gave me a knowing side glance before he cautioned, "Keep that area clean and stay off of those rolling death traps." I smiled back at the doctor.

My knees buckled at the thought that I had just been rescued by two caring humans within the span of an hour. My gratitude was more overwhelming than the shock of the injury. I unhooked B.J. from her shady spot in the foyer and hugged her until she broke free and trotted to the car. She wanted to get me home.

The numbing shock had worn off by the time I entered the cabin. Pain and panic had taken its place.

"Hello, may I speak to Dr. Laura? Tell her it's Jeaninne, her tenant." I felt like vomiting.

"Jeaninne? What's up? Are the animals okay?" Laura sounded concerned.

I lost it. Through my sobs, I relayed the whole embarrassing incident.

"I'll be home soon. I can't believe that doctor didn't prescribe antibiotics for such large surface wounds extremely susceptible to infection. I'll bring you some antibiotics and check for a concussion."

"Thank you so much, Laura. You have been so kind to B.J. and me." I took six Ibuprofen before I collapsed on the green velvet couch under a blanket, my girls spooning into me.

Laura not only checked on me that day, she showed up at my door every morning for a week, applying antiseptic creams and changing my bandages. I met her each day at the door before work, dropping my undies and flashing her a full moon. It became our private joke.

As for Becky, my potential Little Sister, the agency called me soon after the accident to tell me that they found her a male mentor. I packed away my skates and dropped out of the Big Sister program.

Four years later, I ran into Becky working at Burger King. She gave me a lingering glance of recognition. I smiled through my order as if I had never seen her in my life. Sometimes, it's better to let a sleeping dog lie with its owner's roller blades tucked safely away in the back of a dark closet, rather than scare the beast with bloody open wounds.

B.J. snapped me out of my stroll down memory lane by nudging my bare leg with her wet nose. How could I tell Laura goodbye? Leaning on the white wooden fence, I watched the sleek Arabian horses gallop back and forth on their grassy carpet of sunlight. Lined up in military fashion around the fenced-in fields, the towering pines stood at attention. I almost saluted. My future looked optimistic, but my heart felt heavy.

As soon as I heard Laura drive into her carport, I hit her with the news.

"Jeaninne, I can't believe the timing of this! I was trying to find a way to tell you that I will be living between two places. My fiance wants me to move to Carmel with the stipulation that I can keep my business and ranch until I find suitable buyers. Maybe this Victorian house in Lincoln is meant to be part of your life's journey."

"Oh Laura, what a relief. I was feeling guilty, second-guessing my decision to move. B.J. and I will miss you and Tybo terribly, not to mention the beauty and serenity of this ranch. You don't know how much I've appreciated these past four years and all that you've done for us. I had given up hope for a safe, affordable place for me and my girls, not to mention finding the perfect veterinarian for them. Your friendship has been so wonderfully unexpected, yet so necessary for my recovery from a sad divorce. You've helped me move on." My tears symbolized the gratitude and love I felt for Dr. Laura and her furry friends.

"Likewise, Jeaninne. You've been there for Tybo, and many of my animals, when I couldn't be. As a landlord, it's hard to find reliable, trustworthy people like you. Now, dry those tears. Our friendship doesn't end here." We stood under her carport and hugged for several minutes.

Freed up from worry, I began the process of moving. It took a few weeks to sift through, discard, and consolidate my belongings into a small mound of boxes.

Chuck moved my furniture the last weekend in July. I scrubbed windows, floors, and walls until the cabin sparkled. I left it perfect for Laura. B.J. spent most of her time outside with Tybo because change is scary, even for the most stoic among us. Boogers hid under the bed.

Chuck and I packed up in one day, loading up our vehicles and making many runs back and forth to the Lincoln house. With each trip up and down the mountain, my excitement grew. I would have more time to devote to my girls in a more spacious home. Chuck's children met us at the Lincoln house to help me arrange my furniture and to help carry boxes into their proper rooms.

Being their great-grandparents' home, they respected the space and how they handled my belongings. I treated everyone to pizzas and sodas, driving back to the ranch just before dark. I needed to be alone with my girls for our last night in Grass Valley.

Our last night in the cabin tasted bittersweet. We left B.J. to play with Tybo all day while we moved the furniture. I didn't call her in right away. Surrounded by an overnight backpack, a sleeping bag, and pet supplies, I sat in the middle of the bare living room exhausted. Every joint in my body ached. Boogers wouldn't leave my side, proof that she knew our existence in this cabin was already in the past.

"It's okay, Bookish Mishtookus, tomorrow, you'll find everything again in our new home." Boogers curled in my lap. I dozed off to the soothing sound of her soft motor. I left the front door open, waiting for B.J. to join us. I woke to the sound of her paws prancing on pea gravel as she trotted from the barn to the porch, bidding Tybo a good night bark.

Once B.J. saw Boogers and me sitting on the carpeted floor of the barren living room, she stopped as if she had hit an invisible shield pulled across the doorway. She looked at us, and then she looked all around the empty room. B.J. looked clearly confused by the change.

216

Her face said it all: *Where in God's name did everything go?* My funny girl gave me the humor I sorely needed in that moment. She walked in on cat feet and folded in my lap. B.J.'s sudden confusion became my sadness. Our time at the ranch with Dr. Laura and Tybo had reached an end.

The three of us huddled together in the sleeping bag after eating leftover pizza. I wanted to be awake for most of our last night on the ranch, savoring more memories.

However, I fell into a deep sleep before I finished saying the words, "Good night, my loves. Our new life awaits."

CHAPTER TWENTY-TWO

LINCOLN

Chuck and Julie's family home faced east on a large corner lot adjacent to Old Town Lincoln. My nephew once described Lincoln as "Mayberry-like," in reference to the small southern town in the early 1960's television series, "The Andy Griffith Show." This one-hundred-year-old Victorian reeked of history and charm. As only one of three houses on the entire block, it stood uniquely attractive and well-manicured. As much as I missed Laura's ranch, I fell madly in love with this regal beauty.

From the street, the gray and maroon house looked smaller than its actual 1,400 square feet. A pitched roof, outlined in white fretwork with maroon trim, gave the gray home an inviting facade from a bygone era. It reminded me of the American Midwest at the turn of the 20th century when people sat on their porches and drank lemonade. I imagined the men, embroiled in lively discussions regarding the latest trends in farming, sitting at opposite ends from the women who shared baking recipes.

A white wooden railing wrapped around the small porch, big enough for a few over-sized rocking chairs. Two imposing ash trees flanked the front of the house giving it a sense that it was once the only house in the middle of a sprawling farm almost a century ago.

A strip of grass separated the house from the sidewalk. The porch, elevated above the tiny front yard by three broad cement steps, allowed for a bit more privacy. A floor-to-ceiling bay window, split into three panes, bathed the porch in light emanating from the inside of the house.

I grew accustomed to watching pedestrians out of those windows, often many of my students, from my antique rocking chair in the living room. A wooden screen door covered the original, intricately carved front door painted maroon to match the trim. I had moved into a life-sized doll house.

The inside of this landmark home held the magic. Upon entering, a large living room with vaulted ceilings and the original wood floors spread out to the right. To the left, two tandem bedrooms sat adjacent behind French doors.

The first bedroom received the light from the picture window facing the street. The second bedroom, separated by another set of French doors, sank down one step with its own row of high windows running along the south side of the house. I used the first bedroom as a TV room, the second one was reserved for guests.

An imposing stone fireplace owned the center of the living room on the north side of the house. Whoever built the fireplace inserted a colorfully carved clay sun placed between the stone and the wooden mantle.

B.J., Boogers, and I spent many winter evenings huddled under a blanket on my green velvet couch in front of that fireplace, admiring its artistic beauty.

The dining room was separated from the living room by a half wall, giving both rooms the look of an open floor plan. Chuck and Julie had left their grandfather's oak dining table, ornate and formidable, as the focal point of the house. The dining room walls filled the space with built-in glass cabinets for fine China, popular when the house was built. I used them for my pottery pieces.

A spacious bathroom, with a claw-foot tub and large rectangular windows from tub level to the top of the vaulted ceiling, was accessed from the right side of the dining room. That bathroom was my sanctuary. On hot summer days, Boogers sprawled out on the cool porcelain floor of the tub. On cool winter days, I soaked in it for hours, meditating on the towering ash trees that lorded over the backyard.

My room, the master bedroom, was to the left of the dining room as you entered the house. It had its own master bathroom, added a few years before I moved in. Expansive windows welcomed the trajectory of the sun along the south side of the house. Only this room and the guest room were carpeted. Most of the house retained the majesty of the original wood floors.

The kitchen and the sunroom lined up across the back of the house. The sunroom's wall of windows washed the kitchen in light through a French door that separated the two rooms. Boogers shared the sun room with the breakfast nook table. It was the perfect place for her cat box, water, and food dishes. I fed B.J. on the back porch. From the lone kitchen window, the scenic back yard filled my vision when I did the dishes.

The grassy back yard flowed out from the six steps that descended off the small back porch. Ash and Maple trees supplied much needed shade. A large pond broke up the rectangular shape of the yard, giving it a more natural landscape. An eight-foot, gray wooden fence insured privacy.

The yard butted up against an alley used by delivery trucks for the small businesses established on the block behind. Since there was no garage, two wooden storage sheds sat in each back corner. Even this bucolic back yard looked like something from Andy Griffith's Mayberry.

My eclectic antique furniture and treasured art pieces fit in this home as if they were custom-made for it. I worked furiously that first week in the house charged with an unabashed energy to make it my own. I unpacked, decorated, and pounded nails from sun-up to midnight until I dropped from exhaustion each day. I was so busy, I didn't notice B.J.'s imperceptible changes.

The day we left the ranch, B.J. and Boogers acted nervous and confused. The last night proved hard on all of us. Sleeping on the floor without our belongings felt like purgatory, that empty place between our past and our future.

Tears clouded my view when I loaded my girls into the Daihatsu jeep. We would never return as renters. Laura left for the day to give us a smooth leave without having to tear B.J. away from Tybo. I could not survive another goodbye.

As we drove down the gravel road, I watched the horses galloping in the fields through my rear view mirror. B.J. sat up straight when we passed the house with the menacing German Shepherds. Her nostrils expanded as she inhaled their specific scent; her body twitched, probably the muscle memory of dropping to the ground in a submissive position to protect me from possible attacks. B.J. experienced her own memories.

My move to Lincoln, where I had already been teaching for twelve years, happened at the cusp of the biggest Northern California housing boom since the Gold Rush of 1849. In 1993, Lincoln, a sleepy town with tens of thousands of acres of farm land spread out at the base of the Sierra foothills, was known for cattle ranching, the Sierra Pacific lumber mill, and the world renown Gladding McBean pottery factory. At that time, the population hovered around 2,500 compared to the 50,000 it is today.

Even though I cherished the house, I worried that I would hate small town life, especially since I had grown up in fast-paced Southern California. Furthermore, I had previously spent nine years in quaint, art colony resort towns. Surprisingly, Boogers and I adjusted quite well to the slower living pace.

Not B.J.

I was slow to notice the change in her. We established our routine immediately. Once I arranged the house to fit my aesthetic tastes, I concentrated on finding a new running route for B.J. and me. We ran a few blocks behind our house, across the main street through town, over the railroad tracks, and onto a major road leading away from town. When we passed the lumber mill, we looped back through established neighborhoods, and then back home. I timed our runs so that we could watch the sun set beyond the horizon of the outlying, open lands.

What a luxury to be able to arrive home from work early enough to run before nightfall. I gained two more hours without that long commute chipping away at my time and money. However, B.J. seemed to take my lead without her usual enthusiasm. She didn't wait for our runs at the door wagging her tail. Rather, she waited for me to open the door before she gathered up enough energy to get up and follow me.

She also refused to be in the yard alone, whimpering at the back door without me. I rationalized these mood swings to a normal transition period that effect people and animals when their lives change overnight.

B.J. continued to be my teacher's aide at the same school, so that part of her life did not change. The children who lived on the other side of the dirt lot to the north of our house came by often to play with B.J. in the yard. On August 28th, 1993, I invited them over for B.J.'s tenth birthday celebration, complete with cake, party hats and whimsical party favors. She returned to her puppyhood around children. I assumed B.J's lethargy was due to missing the ranch and her old pal, Tybo.

I purposefully kept her close to me, never leaving her alone. So much had happened in the span of our ten years together, I forgot that the years were piling up on her. It seemed that the hair on her muzzle turned gray overnight.

Boogers found her passion in the back yard pond. She often sat staring into the bracken water, hunting for frogs and water bugs. B.J. showed no interest in the pond, and that's when I began to worry. B.J. lived for water, in any form.

"How about a trip to Lake Tahoe this weekend, Beej? I think you need a long swim before the school year begins." Her eyes opened wide in response.

Boogers flipped her tail at us when we locked her in the house on our way out for our Tahoe beach day. She laid in wait to explore the many nooks and crannies this big house offered. I imagined her skidding across the polished floors chasing imaginary rodents, jumping from one high cabinet to another.

I even expected to find a broken pot upon our return. I wouldn't have minded. I wanted both my girls to feel rooted in our new home.

Just like every other time on that Tahoe City beach, B.J. flourished. I didn't make her wait for my command. She flew out of the car and ran to the water, looking back at me for approval. I had not seen her this energized since her time on Dr. Laura's ranch.

"Okay, girl, go for it!" I didn't reel her in from her swim past the shoreline. B.J. came back on her own after endless laps in her happy circle between the swimmers and the tourist boats. When she dropped down next to me, I savored the feel of her silky curls drying in the sun and the smell of fishy lake water on her pink skin.

I snapped a picture of that day, capturing the sun, surf, and my golden girl. I prayed that B.J. would bounce back.

After our beach day, I breathed a little easier. Chuck returned for frequent visits. We weren't dating anymore, but his presence made me feel grounded. He appreciated being welcomed in his grandfather's home on a drop-in basis. B.J. sidled up to Chuck for his special pets, she still felt their close bond. I enjoyed those easy times with Chuck.

"Jeaninne, you've made this house a gorgeous home. It feels cozy with your loving care. It's hard to find good tenants. My sister knew what she was doing when she asked you to rent. Come here, B.J. Give me a hug." Chuck's light blue eyes, burrowed in his tanned leather face, lit up around B.J. He never forgot her kindness during one of his darkest bipolar episodes.

"Thank you for being such a loyal friend, Chuck. This transition hasn't been easy for me and my girls, but something tells me it was the right decision." I slipped into the kitchen to get us a cup of coffee. I didn't want Chuck to see my cry.

"I like having you here, Jeaninne. It makes me feel secure." He followed me to the kitchen, but I kept my back to him while pouring our coffees.

"I feel the exact same way, Chuck." I turned around and accepted his hug.

CHAPTER TWENTY-THREE

*E*DUCATOR

B.J. never accepted her new life in town, but she rallied to the cause for me. I noticed more changes in her behavior. She continued to dislike being in the yard alone. The neighborhood children told me that she howled if I left her outside, for even a half hour, when I did quick errands around town. That broke my heart.

"Okay, girl, from now on, I'll leave you in the house, or you're coming with me, like I promised you after that storm when you ran away from Dr. Laura's ranch." B.J. thumped a paw on my knee while shaking her tail in an even rhythm, swish, swish, swish. I saw a bit of sadness if I looked in her eyes long enough. Her sorrow became my sorrow.

B.J.'s advancing age, coupled with her years of living in nature, made this adjustment even harder. When I kissed the gray hairs around her mouth and wiped her watery eyes, I imagined her saying to me, *How can anyone enjoy being free behind an eight-foot fence you can't see through? It's not natural.*

I responded with a hug and the only words that gave us both comfort, "Mommy loves you." No one could have prepared me for the figurative Half Dome cliff we would soon climb.

Without climbing gear.

B.J.'s greatest joy remained in my classroom with the children. By the time we moved to Lincoln, I had twenty-six Special Day Class students with one aide and no prep time, unheard of for today's Special Day Classes.

Now, a typical class like this has teacher prep time, a few aides, and no more than fifteen students. The stress of behavior management with highly volatile preteens can be a deal breaker for most teachers. But no one else had B.J. She made my teaching days bearable and consistently worthwhile.

In 1990, the district moved me from the back portable to the front corner of the school, once used as office spaces when the school was built in the middle of the 20th century. I had to leave Ben's study cubicles behind because they could not fit in this permanent structure, walled off into two separate rooms with a kitchen and bathroom. The portable classroom was needed to house students in the Resource Specialist Program. I was pleased the cubicles would continue to be useful for other children with learning difficulties before the day we watched them being hauled off for scrap lumber a few years later.

Glen Edwards Middle School was scheduled for classroom renovations the summer of 1993. My room, scheduled to be finished by the time school started in the fall, fell down the list a few months away from completion, after the children returned. I used other people's classrooms during their prep periods, which was an impossibility for teaching behaviorally frustrated, Learning Disabled students.

My supplies remained stacked into 80 boxes in a vacant storage room, so I didn't have access to my materials. In essence, I had to beg, borrow, and steal empty rooms and supplies for my students. My lifelong migraine headaches surged with a vengeance.

My frustrated learners needed, at the very minimum, a learning environment that was engineered to be predictable, stable and routine. Nothing about my situation that fall established a reassuring environment, not even for well-adjusted middle school children. Yet, B.J.'s ability to comfort children experiencing emotional melt-downs saved my days from complete disaster.

At least a half a dozen times a day, I sent B.J. out to the field with an agitated child. The children learned that they had to keep her on a leash close to them as she was also vulnerable; in B.J., they found a kindred spirit. She taught them unconditional love and respect. Rejuvenated from those walks, the students came back with a contented dog trotting faithfully beside them. I truly believe B.J.'s purpose in the classroom kept her from giving up after I pulled her away from the ranch.

⌒

(There are no accidents in a grateful life. After twenty-five years away from my time at the middle school, I am currently coaching a new teacher from the California mandated Teacher Induction program whose classroom is one of the ones I used before my old office room was renovated in 1993. Each week, I walk those familiar hallways feeling B.J.'s presence. For the duration of the nine years I taught at the middle school, she was by my side. B.J.'s work as an educator has been published in a middle school journal and two book anthologies. As I write, that corner classroom is being bulldozed to make way for a new, state-of-art middle school.)

On a Friday, the edict came down from the district office that I could start teaching from my newly renovated classroom the following Monday. In fact, if I didn't move in over the weekend, I wouldn't have any available classrooms to use. I felt as though I had been hit by a Mack truck.

My principal offered no solution as to how I would complete that herculean task. Most teachers have a summer to set up a classroom when the custodians, not the teachers, move the furniture. No one was available for me that weekend.

I called my union rep for answers. He said, "You have the right to ask for extra pay. I will put in a requisition for you."

That didn't help my stress migraines, nor did it solve my time crunch.

I was devastated that Friday after school with a mountain to move ahead of me, so I called Chuck, who had recently retired from the district.

"How am I going to unpack all of those boxes and arrange the furniture by Monday?" I wanted to break glass against my stone fireplace.

Chuck asked, "You mean, the school isn't going to move your things into the room?"

"Yes, but the custodians were dumping furniture and 80 boxes in the middle of the room when I left today, leaving it for me to put away. What am I going to do?"

"Listen, I'll round up three or four of my kids from the high school tennis team to help you tomorrow. Offer to pay them twenty bucks a piece so they show up."

That's exactly what I did. I had no other choice.

In order to celebrate being back in my own room, with my own supplies and my own festive bulletin boards, I proposed that we turn the classroom into a café, making breakfast for the folks who had always supported my program. My students loved the idea! We brainstormed a name for the café. The children unanimously voted for "B.J.'s Café."

Within a day, we had planned the food, the menus, the decorations, and job assignments. I hadn't experienced this much excitement since I first brought B.J. into my classroom. B.J. and I needed a way to connect with the kids after such a hard start to the year. Again, the Beej became our muse.

My fabulous aide, Carol, volunteered to oversee the cooks so that I could manage the cafe. She and I provided the food. Since our room had a mini kitchen, it was the perfect set-up for an electric fryer, a toaster, and a microwave. The students made the menus out of file folders with drawings of B.J. on the covers. The waiters and waitresses wore white shirts and black pants. The cooks sported cook hats and long aprons; the hostesses donned their Sunday best. We even made a sandwich board in the front of the classroom to advertise the daily specials. I decorated the tables with checkered tablecloths, accentuated with multicolored wild flowers the students had picked along their way to school. B.J. served as our mascot, hanging around the cooks who sneaked her bites of bacon.

The morning of the breakfast, every child manned his and her stations before the first bell rang. I escorted in the superintendent, assistant superintendent, principals and school secretaries. B.J. greeted them with a paw shake. When I stepped back to view the café unfolding, my chest filled with pride for my well-behaved students. The hostesses smiled, gave out menus, and seated the guests. The waiters and waitresses spoke clearly and wrote down the orders, even though it was a set menu. The cooks worked quickly to get the scrambled eggs, bacon, toast, and fruit to the tables still warm. When our guests left, the students enjoyed their own feast. Their breakfast table conversations buzzed with the pride they felt from creating such a successful event.

I recently found the pictures, menus, and thank you cards in the garage from "B.J's Cafe." B.J. was in every picture sitting proudly next to each student. I'd be willing to bet that no one who was in attendance that day has forgotten how B.J. helped to reboot our year after its disastrous start.

Sometimes, it's those mishaps that teach us our greatest lessons in life. One lesson I will take to my grave: Support animals make the difference between hope and hopelessness.

My lifelong passion for writing blossomed that year. B.J.'s healing presence in the classroom proved to be therapeutic. I understood that B.J. offered something unique for educators and students alike. I felt compelled to share her story with other educators.

So, I wrote "The Golden Rule" about how B.J. transformed lives in my middle school Special Education classroom. The California Middle School Journal published it in 1993. My girl deserved to be recognized for teaching me to be a better educator, and more importantly, a better person.

Soon after that article was published, I enrolled in a grant writing class. I expanded my passion to write for educational purposes, thanks to B.J., and submitted a grant to Wells Fargo in San Francisco. With the several thousand dollars granted to me by the Wells Fargo headquarters, I hired a counselor for my most disturbed children, giving them a place to be themselves without punishment or reprisal.

My last class, 1993-94, at Glen Edwards Middle School, congealed into a magical, educational elixir—B.J. and I gave my students the best of us. That is all any good teacher, and her canine companion, can hope to accomplish.

CHAPTER TWENTY-FOUR

THE IDES OF MARCH

After seven months, B.J. finally accepted her life in
Lincoln. Resuming her position in my classroom as a
mental health support dog helped to revive her flagging spirit.
She took her role as the resident "counselor" very seriously.
B.J. spent many hours allowing upset adolescents lead her for
tearful walks around the campus. She had a purpose, it showed
in her excitement each morning to ride with me to work. She
couldn't wait to be with *her* students.

B.J. stayed longer in the yard without showing signs
of anxiety. I hung out with her, reading in my beach chair,
savoring our shared time in the sun. Even Boogers encouraged
B.J. to play with her in the pond.

Spring arrived with an abundance of hope—my career advanced as a district grant writer and mentor teacher, B.J. and Boogers settled into our Lincoln home, and the sunny Tahoe ski slopes, dusted in a sparkling powder, waited to be skied upon. I hadn't felt this lighthearted in months. I had my career, my girls, and a nice home.

In the spring of 1994, Laura invited us to an Easter party on her ranch. I was hesitant to take B.J. because I dreaded pulling her away from Tybo, again. Knowing how joyful she would be to see her old friends, I decided to gamble on the fact that it would be a positive choice for my aging girl.

"B.J., Dr. Laura sent us an invitation to an Easter party. How would you like to see Tybo?" I hesitated to say his name. I wasn't sure if I was setting her up for another disappointment.

B.J. sat up from her curled position on my raspberry flowered reading couch and cocked her head. She hadn't forgotten her old friend.

"I know, won't it be fun to see Dr. Laura and Tybo?" I felt like dancing.

She settled in my lap, licking my arm.

"Okay, then it's a go. We're going to dress up in our finest Easter attire and dazzle everyone! Mommy loves you so much."

Something about that moment felt bittersweet. A breeze blew in and gave me the chills.

Once we turned into the gravel road from Highway 174 in Chicago Park, B.J. strained her head out of the open window. Her nose twitched and flared, taking in the scents of those aggressive German Shepherds, the woodsy Ponderosa pines, and the faint sweat of Laura's Arabian horses wafting through the afternoon breezes.

B.J. knocked me out of the car to get to her friends before I could turn off the engine. Laura ran to us, smothering us in bear hugs. Tybo and B.J. rolled in the red dirt, as if no time had passed.

B.J. and Tybo played all day, thrilled to be reunited. I was able to enjoy Laura's guests, delicious arrays of finger foods, and fond memories of my time on the ranch. From Laura's living room window, holding my porcelain tea cup, I noticed the slanted light of the late afternoon sun shining through the giant pines. I inhaled the familiar smell of horses, feeling extremely grateful that B.J. and I had weathered so much in our ten years together. Wiping away a tear, I looked out to see my happy girl romping around the barn with her comical buddy.

Laura visited each guest for a few minutes after dinner. As we enjoyed an array of dainty bakery delights seated from various couches and chairs in her living room, Laura made the rounds, thanking her favorite people for coming to her spring celebration.

"Jeaninne, you don't know how good it is to see you and B.J. Tybo and I have missed you so much. B.J. looks adorable in her tulip scarf. I love your flouncy turquoise dress. You two look like spring goddesses." Laura looked radiant. She wore a flowered summer dress that hugged her perfect figure. Her blonde bob framed her flawlessly tanned face. Even her guests beamed from the reflection of her glow.

I helped Laura clean the kitchen, thankful for a few more stolen moments with her. "Oh, Laura, it seemed like B.J. would never get over missing you, Tybo, and the ranch. I even debated bringing her today, but now I see how happy this visit has made her. I think we are past the worst of so many changes in our lives. I feel like we can breathe again." I even believed the words I spoke.

Laura hugged me. "Jeaninne, I'm so happy for you. We are at a good place in our lives. I'm in a good marriage and I adore our life in Carmel. I have a buyer for the practice. I plan to run my own mobile veterinary truck, so that we can have more time to travel. I'm not sure I want to sell this house. I enjoy coming back to hosts events. Well, let's get back to the party,

I want to show all my friends the new baby goats in the barn."
Laura's attention returned to her guests.

I hung back from the group to spend a little time with
Tybo and B.J. in front of our old cabin. I didn't dare look into
the picture window to see evidence of the new renter, who,
thankfully, was not at home. I noticed that Johnny Doe still ate
the flowers off of the bushes around the porch. It was strange
not to see my hummingbird feeder hanging on the porch, nor
my stained-glass seascape sunlit in the window.

Tybo jumped on my legs, jolting me out of my thoughts.
He and B.J. were playing tug of war with a tree branch. When
Tybo ran to greet me, B.J. stole the branch, then hid around
the corner. Laughter rumbled from the pit of my stomach and
exploded out of my mouth until a bout of hiccups took my
breath away. I wanted to bottle that magnificent day. A slight
sense of dread tugged at me. I swallowed that dark feeling and
jogged back to the party.

⌒

I invited Chuck's sister, Julie, and her husband, Alan, to
dinner soon after Laura's party so they could see what I had
done to her grandfather's house. Chuck visited several times,
but his sister wanted to give me time to settle in before she
visited. I was excited to show my gratitude with the people

243

who had given me this wonderful opportunity to be so close to work. I left school earlier than usual that day to tidy up and fix Chuck's favorite tacos. Before my guests arrived, I fed B.J.

She wouldn't eat.

"What's wrong, Sweetie? You've never turned down a meal." My heart banged hard against my chest.

B.J. looked up at me apologetically. She dropped her head down to the bowl, sniffed at her food, and then walked to the back door with her tail dragging in defeat.

"I understand. You probably have a tummy ache from that bacteria-filled, petri dish of a pond. I'm surprised Boogers isn't sick as well." I let her out minutes before the doorbell rang.

Julie saw the worry in my eyes when she and her husband entered the house. I tried to hide my deep concern for B.J. because I wanted a joyful evening.

"Oh Jeaninne, the house is so artistic, so you. I smell something delicious. Are you alright?" I took their coats and hung them on the coat rack in my bedroom.

"Of course, Julie. Everything is fine. I'm a bit concerned about B.J. She didn't eat tonight. She always inhales her food, morning and night. It's probably the pond water. When we sunbathed last weekend, Boogers and B.J. splashed around in the pond, looking for bugs. I bet it's just an upset tummy." *Oh Lord, please let it be an upset tummy.*

Alan said, "We can check the levels of algae in the pond." *Bless you, dear man.*

"That would be great. Thanks." I gave him a light kiss on his cheek.

Julie made a beeline to the back door to bring B.J. inside. She and Alan showered B.J. with hugs and kisses. They appreciated all B.J. had done for Chuck.

The evening flowed as planned. My tacos tasted every bit as good as they did when my mother made them. Julie and Alan complimented me on my style and hospitality; I so appreciated intelligent, lively conversation with people whom I admired. I even felt a bit better about B.J. because she loved having her friends spoil her with affection. She curled up close to our feet under the antique dining room table throughout the meal.

Standing at the door to say our goodbyes, Julie hugged me. "Please let us know what you find out about B.J. Alan will send someone to check the pond tomorrow." I mustered up a healthy smile. I didn't want these good people to worry more than necessary. Julie knew how much B.J. meant to her brother.

Julie and Alan crouched down to B.J.'s level and gave her words of support that everything would be fine. B.J. rolled over on her back for belly rubs.

B.J. didn't eat the next morning. I coaxed her with an "Ol' Roy" peanut butter dog biscuit. She managed to finish it, tentative bite after tentative bite.

I drove into my parking spot filled with sorrow. My instincts told me that something was terribly wrong with my girl. I couldn't think any further than that moment because the possibilities felt like a tsunami wave hovering over me, ready to crash. I vowed to stay strong and do whatever I needed to fix her. I acted immediately.

I marched into the principal's office and announced, "Barbara, I never, ever take days off. I'm here from sunrise to sunset every day, right? Well, now it's my turn to ask for a favor. I need to take B.J. to the Loomis Basin Vet Clinic today. I booked an appointment for 1:00 p.m. I already called for a half-day sub." I explained B.J.'s lethargy and sudden loss of appetite.

"Jeaninne, you don't need to justify your decisions. We all love B.J. and want the best for both of you. I'm glad you're tending to her needs." Barbara squeezed my hand.

That tsunami knocked me down until I felt like I was drowning.

"I can't live without her, Barbara. I can't. I know I'm overreacting, but she's my everything. Thank you so much for understanding." Barbara hugged me tight like a mother worried about her child.

The students distracted B.J. that day with their usual attention, but she lost the prance in her step. I threw myself into my teaching because it kept me sane when Ben left. I loved my students and always wanted the best for them. Even in times of distress, my students were number one when I was at the helm of my classroom.

I told my class about B.J.'s loss of appetite. My students loved their golden girl; she was their teacher, too. They deserved the truth. The children circled B.J. with hugs and kisses before we left for the vet's office. She responded with paw thumps and wet kisses.

The children gave me the faith I needed that all would end well. That blind innocence kept me from giving up.

CHAPTER TWENTY-FIVE

WONDER WOMAN

After B.J. and I raced from school to get to her 1:00 p.m. appointment, I was relieved for the few minutes we had to cuddle in the fairly empty waiting room.

An elderly woman sat in the corner by the aquarium so her fat cat could watch the fish from his carrier. B.J. laid across my lap, shaking with fearful anticipation. A petite woman in a white coat called our names, instructing us to follow her.

"We need to take blood tests. I can't assess the situation until we know what we're dealing with," said the taciturn female doctor who had none of Dr. Laura's charm.

"When will we know?" I stroked B.J.'s head, pouring my healing energy into each one of those caresses.

"I will hurry the results. I can see you're anxious." That was an understatement.

"Thank you. What about her appetite? She has to eat."

"Find whatever foods B.J. likes. You may resort to people food to stimulate her appetite. It's only been a day. It's more important she drinks plenty of water."

I left that clinic, touted as one of the best in Northern California, with a half a heart.

I kept B.J. home from school for the following day. She needed to rest in the house with Boogers for much needed peace and quiet, at least until we knew how to proceed.

We didn't do our usual evening run. Instead, I walked her a few blocks around the town. B.J. and I must have looked like xeroxed copies of ourselves, withered and faded.

The phone rang as I crawled into bed. I had forgotten about the outside world.

"Hi Jeaninne. Julie told me about B.J. Alan got the results back from the pond. There are no worrisome algae or bacteria counts, at least nothing that can harm pets. How's she doing?"

Chuck's voice soothed my restless soul.

"Well, Chuck, she's trying to be stoic because she knows I'm sad. She was great with the children today. I fixed her some boiled chicken and rice after we returned from the clinic, but she only picked at a few bites. Normally, as you know, she would have devoured that special meal like a vacuum cleaner. Even our walk was listless. I'm scared." I was petrified.

"Listen, if you need anything, I mean anything, I'm here." *What a great friend you are, Chuck.*

"And that means everything to me. Thank you, Chuck."

I tucked B.J. in under the high bed Ben built out of logs. Boogers slept burrowed into my stomach. We slept like the dead. The next day, I left campus at lunch to get the blood results. I assured my compassionate principal that I would be back in time when the bell rang for class to begin.

The same female vet saw me right away. "It appears B.J. has cancer, but we will have to do more tests to determine which kind."

My mind faded to black. I felt sick.

"What do I do?" The room spun around like a bad scene in a horror film.

"She has cancer. What else can you do?" *Did this doctor really deliver a death sentence like a surly teen?*

I fantasized jumping across the stainless steel table, slapping that smug look off her face. That woman gave my girl a death sentence before we knew anything definitive. I ran out of that office before I said, or did, anything I would later regret.

I made it back to class just in time. I shared my anger with my students who were equally incensed. We all missed B.J. I regretted not bringing her to class. We carried on as usual, but I knew that my usual had vanished with B.J.'s appetite. I had no idea what would happen next; that frightened me the most.

While boiling chicken for B.J., I made a call that would change my mood from hopeless to hopeful.

"Laura, it's Jeaninne." I relayed every detail of B.J.'s current health status and that insensitive doctor's dismissive attitude.

"What should I do now, Laura? I'm literally beside myself. I can't even think."

"I was leaving with my honey for an event in Carmel; however, if you bring B.J. up to my hospital now, I will do whatever it takes to find answers. We can fly his jet later this evening after I assess our girl." I loaded B.J. in the car. We arrived within an hour.

Laura greeted us in a black sequined evening gown, looking like a movie star; her hair, a glowing halo of spun silk, had the look of messy elegance. She smelled like Jasmine on a warm summer's eve. I cried ugly tears into her white doctor's coat. B.J. leaned into her side.

"Leave B.J. here overnight for tests. Go home and get some sleep. We'll hook her up for intravenous nutrition. I'll call you when I get the results. You know we all love B.J., so stop worrying, at least for tonight." I couldn't believe this ravishing creature stood before us like Super Woman.

"I love you, Laura." The only words I could retrieve.

I drove home feeling like a zombie, bereft, bloodless, out of my mind. The apocalypse had arrived as far as I was concerned. Nothing but B.J. mattered. Every ounce of me lasered on her care. I couldn't think past the present. I don't even know how I concentrated on my driving, but as soon as I walked into the house to comfort Boogers, I passed out on the bed. The clock ticked 7 p.m.

I woke up in a fog of disorientation when the phone rang at 9 p.m.

"It's Laura. The X-rays and blood work show that B.J. has an enlarged spleen full of infection. If I don't get her into surgery now, that infection could suddenly burst, which would be fatal. I'm going to stay and operate." *God Bless you, Wonder Woman.*

Laura and I cried together over the phone. Our girl faced the fight of her life.

"Jeaninne, this is not related to your care. I know you feed B.J. the healthiest brands and refrain from feeding her table scraps. She's not young anymore. These things happen to older, purebred canines. B.J. is next to me and I see the trust in her eyes. I'll call you in the morning when we know more."

I trust you with my life, Dr. Laura.

I didn't sleep one wink that night, not even enough to dream.

I instructed the school secretaries to transfer Laura's call into my classroom that morning. My students stopped working and looked up at me when the phone rang. I blew them a kiss.

"Jeaninne, B.J. is resting well. I want to keep her here for observation today, and maybe tomorrow. Let's see how she does before I give you a pick-up time. I'm flying to Carmel today, but my staff will keep me informed." The blood rushed back into my extremities.

"Oh Laura, I'm so sorry I ruined your plans last night. But, I'm not sorry you did the surgery. It had to be you. Words aren't sufficient for expressing my gratitude, nothing I can do for you in return is sufficient, but thank you for B.J.'s life."

The children let out a collective cheer, jumping up and down with their arms linked in unity. Their love for B.J. humbled me, reminding me that nothing lasts forever.

"What do you say we go out to the field and play tag? B.J. would love that."

I brought B.J. home after two days of recovery. Like a wounded soldier who returned home with a broken soul, her ebullient spirit died on the battlefield. The switch flipped—I became her caretaker, she could no longer take care of me.

Laura explained that her recovery would be slow. B.J. had major surgery with compounding effects on her other organs. It would take time for everything to function normally without the spleen. I discovered that B.J. could tolerate baby food. Other than going to work, I didn't leave her side.

Throughout her first night home, B.J.'s painful cries cut into me like rusty knives. I removed my bedding and folded out the flowery futon couch onto the floor. I slept by her side, night after night, our whimpers blending as one. I whispered,

"Mommy is here, Mommy loves you, and we will get through this together." I became her legs to get her out the front door to do her business in the side lot. My hope hinged on the outcome of her improvement.

My students missed B.J. in the classroom as much as I did. They made lovely cards that I read to her each night. I cut down on my work hours and shortened my evening runs in order to make sure she had regular outside breaks. Boogers slept by B.J.'s side when I couldn't be there. Bit by bit, her strength returned. However, her lust for life had visibly diminished.

One morning, before I left for work, B.J. didn't have the strength to get up to do her business. I carried her outside. Her shaky legs could barely hold her body upright enough to complete the act of urinating; her bowel movements were next to nothing.

B.J. looked up at me with sorrowful eyes that spoke volumes. *I'm so sorry, Mommy. I'm trying, I really am.*

"I know you are, baby. Please don't worry about me." Each day, a part of me died.

I couldn't leave her unattended for a full day. My mother offered several times to come up and sit with B.J., but she was finishing her last year of work. I didn't want to cut into the sick leave dividends she had purposely saved to augment her retirement benefits. Just knowing Mom was always there for us was immensely comforting. I gave her updates every single day. That particular day, I needed Chuck.

"Hi Chuck. I'm going to take you up on your offer to help. Can you take B.J. up to Mother Gold Hospital today? I called about her increasing fragility. They told me to bring her up as soon as possible. I can't take off work today because I'm doing a special presentation for the district. Her appointment is at 10 a.m." *Oh, please say yes.*

Chuck didn't hesitate. "I'd do anything for B.J."

B.J. was given a new regime of medications. The bile that is normally processed through the spleen was leaking into other organs. Steroids and more effective pain relievers gave B.J. back more of her spunk. Chuck enjoyed his time spent with B.J. that day, paying her back for the love she had given him in his time of need. He took her back to his ranch for a walk along the creek, her favorite place to relax.

By mid-April of 1994, a month after the surgery, B.J. was able to eat small bits throughout the day and stopped crying out in pain each night. I prayed her return to daily child care would give her a reason to fight. It did.

My students realized B.J.'s limitations in the classroom. They walked her, but not out in the back fields. I curtailed the walks to an area outside of the classroom, which was surrounded by the grassy yards that faced the front corner of the school. I watched her from the classroom windows.

Often, B.J. stopped walking and sprawled out on the grass. Her student guide, carrying B.J.'s emergency kit, stretched down next to her to brush her faded fur. Those quiet moments were just as healing for my students as a jog in the field.

I joined a gym in the neighboring town of Rocklin. I switched up our long runs for short walks around town. I still craved the intense exercise that had challenged me for most of my life. B.J. liked accompanying me to the gym where people pet her on their way in and out of the facility.

She didn't mind being tied up on a very long lead, resting in the shaded entryway with her water bowl. I could see her from every angle during my workouts.

We adapted to B.J.'s new normal as best as we could. I even attended a non-denominational congregation on Sundays. I needed to be closer to God so that I had an arsenal of spiritual tools to face anything with respect to B.J.'s tenuous health.

Each time we walked a little further around town, I looked to the sky, convinced that God looked down on us. I said the prayer, "Thank you, God, for giving us this one day. I know it's all we have." I'm far from any kind of religious convert, but I so respect people of faith. In the end, faith is all that remains.

CHAPTER TWENTY-SIX

KITES

From downtown Lincoln, I drove south on Highway 65 for five miles, turning east onto Sunset Boulevard for another five miles, to arrive at my Rocklin gym. At the corner of Highway 65 and Sunset, grassy knolls spread out on either side of the boulevard. A modern industrial park was hidden behind massively tall fir trees that lined one side of the highway's verdant fields. A furniture factory was off in the distance on the other side of the highway. In the spring, groups of people gathered on the lawns with colored kites of every shape, color, size, and theme. Their sky dances calmed me.

"Look, B.J., aren't the kites stunning?" She watched from the back window, setting her sight on one kite—up, down, left, right, around and around. Those kites motivated her to sit up on weak legs. We passed by the kite enthusiasts so many times on our daily gym commute, I was becoming familiar with some of the regulars—parents, children, teens, and adults.

B.J. and I had not experienced any fun since early March, the night Julie and Alan came for dinner. I couldn't believe how fast those two months of sorrow had passed. Had the oppressive fog of B.J.'s illness lifted? Just like the battle of white cumulus clouds fighting against heavy rain clouds above us, I couldn't answer which way B.J.'s health would shift.

Life in the Victorian house resumed a balance I welcomed with open arms of relief. B.J. struggled to get back to her previous level of energy by eating measured portions of high premium dog food throughout the day.

(Thank you "Ol' Roy" peanut butter dog biscuits for keeping her alive).

I couldn't walk her further than a few blocks through town; yet, it was enough to give us both fresh air and continued hope. B.J. tended to the children with ample time to rest in the classroom between lawn walks.

At the end of the day, I had my girls. That was enough.

One kite fan on the northern grassy area caught my attention each time B.J. and I drove to the gym. In a sea of Caucasian faces, a dark, muscular Asian man stood out from the crowd. Sporting a baseball cap and Ray Ban sunglasses, I couldn't see his face, which increased the allure factor.

That late April broke heat records, so the Asian man usually wore a variation of colors on the same clothing theme— tank top, cargo shorts, and flip flops. A long, thick ponytail cascaded down his back which added further intrigue to his unconventional looks. I often saw him crouched down to help a child untangle his or her kite lines, or he stood next to an adult pantomiming the finer points of flying dual line kites. That delicious man exhibited kindness and patience. My curiosity grew into a mission.

"B.J., I bet that gorgeous man is taken. I mean, how could he not be swept up by some lucky lady already. I know, I'm acting like a teenybopper with a crush on a pop star. It's just fun to daydream about the various lives we see flying kites on our drive through these fields."

When I looked back at her, B.J. was also watching the Asian man, who had begun steering his own kite—up, down, left, right, around and around. Looks like we shared the same taste in men.

"Hey Beej, let's walk around the kite fields on Sunday! It will be a nice change of pace and we can watch the colored kites swirling over our heads." She smiled back at me with those half-mast eyes. I imagined her thoughts: *You can't fool me, Mom, you want to meet that mystery man.*

"I admit, it would be nice to casually happen upon him." I winked at her through the rear view mirror.

I waited a week to take B.J. to the kite fields. Julie and Allan invited us to a spring party on their ranch. I wanted to show everyone how much B.J. had improved, and to give her a day of constant attention. Chuck and his children ran to B.J. with warm hugs.

While sitting next to B.J. on Julie's sloping lawn, breathing in the panoramic view of the cows and the great Oaks, a sudden wave of emotion washed over me.

Chuck's children attended college. Julie's children planned to marry. Time marched on. I adored these people for so many reasons, but I realized it was my turn to find my family, my place in the world.

The following Sunday morning, I packed up B.J.'s emergency kit—water, snacks, brush, bed, leash, medications. If we decided to stay a few hours with the kite fliers, I prepared for any health issue that could have reared its ugly head. I hadn't felt this kind of anticipation since we moved to Lincoln.

It was the kind of day Walt Disney captured in his animated films—blue skies, puffy white clouds, melodic birds, and gentle breezes that filled the air with magic.

On May 1st, 1994, we parked at the end of the north field at the corner of Highway 65 and Sunset. B.J.'s nose twitched with the various scents brought in on soft winds. We ambled along in the grass, smiling at the people we often saw from the car. Children of all ages ran up to B.J. with an assortment of hugs.

The proximity of the kites flying above us made me think of park life in the Golden Age of the late 1880's: women cinched into long dresses holding lace parasols; men nattily attired in their top hats and tails walking with gold-tipped canes; girls wearing large hair bows dressed in white pinafores skipping with their friends; and, boys wearing brown knickers with long black socks flying wayward kites. I saw many of these classic paintings during my European sojourns. Old Master painters focused their perspectives on movement through the children they painted. I wanted to paint this day filled with our movements, walking with my golden girl within a colorful blur of swirling kites.

I scanned the field for the Asian man—he was nowhere
in sight. B.J. seemed to sense my disappointment and looked
forlornly into the distance.

"I know you're tired, Sweetie, but let's walk over to the
south field for one last round." I gave her water and a biscuit
outside of the car. Nearing noon under a blazing sun, I ditched
my running jacket and slathered on sunscreen. We looked
both ways before we crossed the four lanes spanning Sunset
Boulevard. B.J. pulled me along as if she were on a mission of
her own.

The only people we witnessed on this opposite field sat
under day tents eating lunch next to parked cars. Not one kite
on this side of the boulevard appeared in the sky.

"It's warm, Beej. What do you say we pack it in for the
day?" I bent down to check her nose for heat exhaustion. Still
moist and cool to the touch, I felt the stirring of a gentle breeze.

When I stood up, I saw a dark figure walking our way. We
stayed on the south corner of Sunset and Highway 65, about
100 yards from the parked cars in front of us. I looked around
to see if this person's attention focused on something else.

Not one other human being inhabited our line of vision.
To our right, the wide boulevard spread into four lanes. To our

left, dirt fields extended past the vast lawn. Behind us, only the whoosh of Sunday traffic on Highway 65.

"B.J., could that be our Asian man?"

The essence of a person came into view as the handsome Asian man wearing a royal blue baseball cap, black Ray Ban sunglasses, white tank top, khaki cargo shorts and Hawaiian print flip flops. *Yes, B.J., it is our man.* "B.J., I think our mystery man has found us." B.J. sat at full attention with her head straining forward.

He said, "What a beautiful dog." *What a beautiful man.*

I looked into the dark Ray Bans that sat on his high cheek bones and blurted out, "I think she's dying."

I never uttered those words, but something about this man made me want to tell him everything. I wanted him to know how long I've held back my tears, my worry, my grief for the eventual end of the only being who has been by my side for almost eleven years, the one soul who saved my life when I wanted to give up. I needed him to know. *Hold back your tears, Jeaninne, now is not the time.*

"Oh no, I'm so sorry. I'm Glenn, by the way." He extended a large warm hand. We shook on our hello as if we were agreeing to be friends for life.

"This is B.J. I'm Jeaninne." I sat down to comfort my girl, hoping she wasn't devastated by my blatant announcement regarding her slow decline. B.J. acted as though she hadn't heard a word. She stared into the soul of this man. Something about him seemed to fascinate her.

Glenn sat on the grass with us. I told him about B.J.'s long health battle. He stroked her back the entire time I talked. B.J. surrendered to his touch and laid her head in his lap. Glenn told me about how he had just lost his German Shepherd mix, Casey. He explained that when he saw us at the end of the field, he immediately felt our connection.

The heat became unbearable, so I excused myself to get B.J.'s emergency kit from the car. When she didn't move to follow me, I let her stay with Glenn. I didn't think twice about leaving her with that familiar stranger. She had already given him her consent.

Glenn suggested we sit on the tailgate of his truck to be out of the sun. I gave B.J. her medicine, more water, and then settled her down in the shade of his pop-up tent. She seemed perfectly content, as if this was where she was meant to be on May 1st, 1994.

We talked about Glenn's upbringing in Sacramento as a Japanese American, his job at Formica Industries in middle management, his desire to seek a career in the California correctional system, and our similar childless marriages.

I stared into his exotic face, noting the high cheek bones, creamy dark skin, brown almond eyes, cupid lips, and board-straight nose. His hair was cinched into a long ponytail at the base of his neck. I could have looked at that face forever.

I told Glenn about my upbringing in Southern California, my teaching career, my divorce, and my love for B.J. When all was shared, the sun had shifted toward the horizon. Hunger pulled me back to reality.

"Wow, what time is it? B.J. and I need to eat." We talked for five hours.

Glenn smiled, shook my hand, and bent down to hug B.J. I hooked my girl to her leash, turned to wave, and jogged back to the car. Dumbstruck, I filled B.J.'s water bowl. A lump formed in my throat as I fought back my tears.

After all that, he didn't even ask for my phone number. I knew he was too good to be true.

I felt cheated. Five hours of devoted conversation with a potential kindred spirit and he didn't ask for my information. Truly disappointed, I brushed B.J's soft coat.

"I liked him, too, girl. I thought he liked us. Oh well, his loss." I hoisted her up into the back seat and belted her in.

After B.J. and I ate at the house, I didn't feel like hopping into the car to go back to the gym. I called my mother, instead. Mom's comfort never failed.

"Hi Mom, something really interesting just happened."

I replayed the day in its entirety. "What do you think I should do? I don't want to chase Glenn if he's not interested, but there was such a palpable connection. B.J. doesn't warm up to strange men with such an immediate trust. It felt like she had known Glenn in another life."

I could bank on my mother's advice. "On your way to the gym, if you see Glenn, pull over and wave. I'm sure he'd like that. Maybe, he didn't want to come on too strong. Did he ask if you and B.J. would return to the field anytime soon?"

"Not that I remember. Mom, I can't ask a man out."

"Honey, Glenn doesn't seem like most men."

I waited four days before I drove to the gym via Highway 65 and Sunset Boulevard. I couldn't bear to see Glenn without knowing where I stood.

CHAPTER TWENTY-SEVEN

GLENN

"I know you want to see him again, Sweetie. So do I. Okay, we'll drive by the fields on the way home from the gym today." B.J. sat up straighter. She knew what "okay" meant. I drove to the gym on the back roads from Lincoln into Rocklin for four days to avoid Glenn. During my workout, I realized that my pride grew into ridiculous proportions. It was time to put on my big girl pants and face my destiny, whatever that meant.

Blinded by the sun as I drove west down Sunset Blvd., I flipped up the visor. I saw Glenn waving his arms at the edge of the kite field. I almost turned right onto Highway 65 before I screeched into the last parking spot along the curb.

Glenn sprinted to my car, a bit out of breath by the time he reached the driver's side. I'd forgotten the perfection of his lean, muscular body.

"Where have you two been?" B.J.'s tail wagged vigorously at the mere sound of his deep, melodic voice. *You would have known if you asked for my number.*

I couldn't lie to that handsome face. "Truth be told, since you didn't ask for my phone number last Sunday, I've been avoiding you. And, how did you know my car?"

Glenn smiled. "I watched you and B.J. get into your Rocky Dihatsu last Sunday. I doubt anyone else would have the license plate, "The Beej." If you didn't drive by the fields this week, I was going to get your number through the Department of Motor Vehicles where my stepbrother works. Hello B.J., I want to show you ladies how to fly a dual line kite." *Or, you could have asked for my number in the first place.*

B.J. jumped out of the back seat and trotted beside Glenn. He clipped on her leash, the two of them walking in front of me as if I weren't even there. *What a sly guy.*

When something works, it flows like water rushing downhill. Accustomed to men like Ben and Chuck laying out conditions, I didn't know what it felt like to be with a man who never questioned anything. With Glenn, I wasn't asked to explain my actions. He accepted me as he found me, a fully-fledged adult woman with all her idiosyncrasies. Even better, he was crazy about B.J.

Our relationship developed at warp speed. The early days blurred into one continuous time frame with no beginning or end. Glenn and I became best friends overnight. B.J. and I spent every day after work flying kites with him. Without expending too much energy from her spot on the grass, B.J. reveled in the attention the kite club members lavished upon her. I knew her health would be forever compromised.

I savored each day she was gifted to me, each day I could share her with the new man in our lives. By the time Glenn and I had our first date to his favorite Japanese restaurant, we already knew most things about each other.

In late May, I asked Glenn if he would like to be my escort for my 8th grade students' graduation ceremony. He accepted without reservation. Ben would have acted uncomfortable in front of my colleagues; Chuck would have respectfully declined, not wanting to publicize our couple status.

Glenn didn't hesitate, "Of course, I would be honored." This amazing man kept checking off the boxes of what I wanted in a life partner.

More important, Glenn felt completely comfortable in his own shoes. He didn't seem own any emotional baggage.

I couldn't wait to parade Glenn in front of my students and colleagues. He appeared on my doorstep in a black suit, dark gray dress shirt, and a purple paisley tie—all 175 pounds of him encased in 5'11" of muscle. With his long hair slicked back in a tight ponytail, he looked like a member of the Japanese Mafia in a blockbuster gangster flick.

I wore a classy red dress that hugged my runner's body, my brown wavy hair cascading down my back. I wanted Glenn to be proud of me. B.J. stood before us grinning from ear to ear. We promised to take her for a walk before sundown.

My students flocked around us before we found our seats in the first row facing the stage. Once Glenn put on his sunglasses, his image seared permanently into my memory bank. He didn't look like anyone else in the audience that night. My face hurt from smiling. I was proud of my man.

Juan Pablo, a rebellious student who often slammed me with obscenities, a student I suspended on a regular basis, bolted into the classroom the next day full of curiosity.

"Miss Escallier, was that your boyfriend at the graduation?"

His normally skeptical smirk turned into a child's curious countenance.

"Yes, that's right, Juan Pablo." I puffed up with pride.

"Does he know karate? He looks like one bad dude." *Is there a hint of fear, J.P.?*

"As a matter of fact, he does. He told me to tell any student who disrespects me that he or she would have to deal with him first. Understand?" *Wow, I do have a boyfriend who would protect me.*

Juan Pablo hesitated before he spoke. "Uh, yeah, I wouldn't want to rumble with that guy." Glenn's influence reached deep. Before his presence in my life, I never dreamed Juan Pablo could grasp the concept of respect.

I turned away so Juan Pablo wouldn't see my laughter. Glenn didn't know karate, nor did he tell me he would defend me from my students. However, I found it a convenient ploy to get through the last week of the school year without any classroom disruptions.

With harmony in my personal life, I wanted to share it with my students.

"Jeaninne, where have you been? I've been leaving messages for almost two weeks." I wasn't ready to tell Chuck. I wanted to keep Glenn to myself.

"Oh, hi, Chuck. Sorry, my life has been crazy with B.J. and the end-of-the-year activities. I haven't been home much." *How am I going to approach this?*

"How's B.J. doing?"

"Well, she's actually had a surge of energy lately. She's not one hundred percent, but her spirits are much better. I need to share with you a big change in our lives."

I told Chuck everything. I could feel the heaviness of his emotions through the earpiece.

A full minute passed before he responded. "Wow, I didn't expect this."

"Neither did I. I'm still not sure it's real." My heart melted, a part of Chuck still loved me.

Chuck's voice became a whisper. "I'm truly speechless. I mean, somewhere deep inside I held out hope that we would have a future together. I don't know what to say."

"Chuck, we haven't been together for two years. You've been dating Mary for a long time."

I reminded him of reality even when he didn't want to face it.

"I know, I know. It's just that when I see you in my grandparents' home, it gives me such a feeling of security, a feeling of permanence. I know I haven't been there for you the way you deserve. I probably bury reality because it's too painful for me to face the truth. You know how I am, you said it yourself, I'm the quintessential Peter Pan."

"Our friendship will never change, Chuck. You were that person who rescued me from a sad, painful divorce. You gave me back my laughter, my spontaneity, my spark, but you didn't give me permanence. Now, it's *my* turn to be happy."

Glenn planned a camping trip along the coast for the end of June with the kite club. He thought B.J. needed time to do her favorite things while she still had some fight left. Glenn borrowed his stepfather's camping trailer, complete with a kitchenette and tiny shower. We packed it up for a long weekend of fun in the sun, a celebration of our love and B.J.'s improvement.

I couldn't believe how quickly my life had changed. At almost forty, I felt like my life had just begun.

One afternoon in late May, after B.J. and I had completed her potty walk in the dirt lot beside our home, she collapsed at the bottom of the front porch steps. I calmed her with a bowl of fresh water, helped her into the house, and then called Laura.

"Laura, I know you're in Carmel, but what should I do?" *Oh God, please, just give her more time with Glenn and me.*

"I'll call my Grass Valley office to tell them you're coming. You need to take B.J. in for further tests."

B.J. refused to eat. She vomited green bile in the car on the way to Mother Gold Veterinary Hospital. Glenn ran over as soon as I called him to tell him that we wouldn't be flying kites that day. He drove so I could be in the back seat with my girl. With her head in my lap, I whispered, "B.J., we still have a new life ahead of us with Glenn. Please hold on." Her eyes held mine. I felt her words. *I will do everything it takes, Mommy, because I want to see you happy before I go.*

I couldn't have coped without Glenn's calming presence.

Glenn carried B.J. into the office. The young veterinarian, Dr. Chris, assured me that B.J. would be hooked up to intravenous feedings to give her back some strength. He encouraged me to leave her overnight. Glenn held my hand all the way home.

My mind, not completely present the next day in the classroom, replayed our life over and over. I was grateful the students were busy finishing final assignments and playing learning games. My teaching year technically ended, so I didn't have to fake my fears behind lofty lessons. During lunch, I called the Mother Gold Veterinary Hospital.

"Hi Jeaninne, B.J. is resting comfortably, but I have some unexpected news. Our technical equipment is limited for what appears to be more complications with the workings of her internal organs. Dr. Laura and I have conferred and we believe you should take B.J. to UC Davis for a complete battery of tests. They have the capability in their teaching hospital to rule out any and all medical doubts."

My heart murmur fluttered. I inhaled deeply to set it right.

I couldn't speak right away.

"Yes, I'm still here. So, how do I do that? I don't know how to start the process. I can't even think right now."

"We will set up the appointment and then call you back. I know this is hard, we all love B.J. Keep positive thoughts that UC Davis can sort this out; and, keep breathing."

Dr. Chris called me back that afternoon before I left school.

"If you can pick up B.J. this evening, UC Davis will admit her tomorrow afternoon by five p.m." Wild horses couldn't keep me away.

"We will be there in a few hours. I have to wait for my boyfriend to get off work. Thank you, doctor." A sudden rush of relief washed over me. Someone who loved me would be by my side.

I suddenly remembered I used the word, boyfriend. With the laser energy I focused on B.J., I forgot to count my blessings. For a few seconds, I allowed myself to smile, feeling grateful my girl approved, and maybe conjured, the wonderful man in our lives.

CHAPTER TWENTY-EIGHT

A SETBACK

B efore Glenn literally walked into our lives, I had begun the process of researching new teaching positions, within and out of the district. I needed a career change. The county and district loaded my class with too many extreme behavioral challenges; my incessant migraines had become physical proof of that stress. I gave my soul to that program for nine years. A new opportunity might bring back balance in my life.

While B.J. awaited her fate, I accepted a teaching job at Phoenix Continuation High School, a few blocks from the middle school. I would teach a few teens with mild learning disabilities and behavioral issues, but the majority of students lacked regular high school credits.

The students received regular high school academics in an individualized configuration via computer and direct, teacher instruction. Each teacher instructed students in a drop-in, more loosely structured manner, tailored made for teens with babies and full-time jobs. Teachers tutored in the afternoons and taught regular classes in the mornings.

I was hired as the English, Drama, and P.E. teacher. Hopeful for this new challenge, I couldn't wait to share B.J.'s teaching expertise with the older students.

The day Glenn and I picked B.J. up at Mother Gold, I couldn't hide the shock at how much weight she lost. The nutrition drips kept her barely alive. Dr. Chris walked us out to the car, looking tired and defeated.

"We're so sorry we can't tell you more, Jeaninne. It appears B.J.'s organs are not working in tandem, but the doctors at the teaching hospital will be able to sort things out with their state-of-the-art equipment. Please keep us informed when you know more. We also alerted UC Davis to send us B.J.'s records. Dr. Laura will be checking in as well. Goodbye sweet B.J." Dr. Chris kissed the top of her head.

I dabbed at my tear-stained face while Glenn carried her to the back seat. She looked so weak and forlorn. My heart hurt. I could feel it crack and shatter within the walls of my chest.

Not unlike the many times I faced loss within the past ten years, I let the tears fall on B.J.'s head tucked into my lap. Glenn remained silent, giving B.J. and I our private time. I whispered words of hope and renewal. "We are here for you, B.J. Whatever happens, our love will get us through anything."

I put B.J. to bed on our futon mattress. Glenn and I slept on either side of her. We faced a turning point the next day. It was time to admit B.J. into the UC Davis Veterinary Hospital. It was time to face the truth.

I left B.J. at home with Boogers, our intrepid Siamese cat, who had been extremely loving and patient with B.J.'s declining health. Boogers kept her eye on B.J. and alerted me with a paw tap to my leg if B.J. cried out in pain, especially during those first days of her illness. Glenn drove straight to my house after work.

The entire school knew B.J. was going to UC Davis and that I was needed at home right after the children left for the day. A flood of love and well-wishes followed me out my classroom door.

Children and dogs, God's angels.

Once we checked in, a team of veterinary students joined us in the foyer to escort B.J. to her room. Their encouraging words affected B.J.'s mood, she wagged her tail as each student cooed in her face. Glenn hoisted her up into his muscular safe arms, also whispering words of comfort. The students surrounded us, giving B.J. sweet pep talks and loving caresses as we walked her back to the observation room.

One of them assured us, "Someone will call you as soon as we know more. And don't worry, B.J. won't be left alone. We can see how much you love her and how much she loves you. Each one of our patients is special to us." That bit of comfort meant so much that day.

We kissed and hugged B.J. I said, "We will be back soon to get you, Sweetie. Mommy loves you…and so does Glenn." Glenn had to gently take me away. I couldn't let go of her.

Again, another interminable wait.

The call came within two days.

"Jeaninne, we have the results of B.J.'s tests." My knees buckled.

"Her kidneys are failing." *Oh God, no.* I felt the room spin before I fell back into a dining room chair.

"So, here's the plan. We're going to give her a full blood transfusion to clean out the infected blood. That should buy you a few more months. You'll know when the healthy blood cells begin to be replaced with sick ones.

B.J. will show signs of weakness, loss of appetite, and depression. Short of giving her a kidney transplant, which is not yet perfected in canines, we must ensure her lust for life is strong. Based on how much she is loved, you should have at least two or three more months of quality time. I wish we could give you better news, but I think you will be pleased with the transfusion." All I heard was "...a few more months."

I called Glenn, and then I cried. My girl had been given an expiration date.

CHAPTER TWENTY-NINE

GOLDEN SUMMER

The doctors gave me the green light to bring B.J. home. Her transfusion worked; she showed no signs of adversity from the procedure. I couldn't concentrate all day at work, my thoughts were focused on holding my golden girl in my arms again. If it weren't for my students' favorite B.J. stories offered up as hopeful prayers, I might have gone mad with worry. I vowed not to think about her future. In fact, all I could think about was kissing her broad, beautiful face.

Glenn and I jogged from the parking lot into the lobby of UC Davis Veterinary Hospital. My heart pounded so loudly with anticipation, I heard the blood pulsing in my ears. Glenn calmly announced our presence at the desk. When he said that we were there for B.J., the receptionist smiled. My girl worked her magic on everyone at UC Davis, like she always did, wherever we went.

We sat on the wooden bench facing the long hallway. I felt like B.J. when her senses locked in on a squirrel that had scurried up one of the pine trees on Laura's ranch. Her body froze with a laser beam focus that shot from her eyes into the body of her furry target. I could feel my body twitching, frozen at attention. With a laser beam focus, I leaned forward, waiting for *my* furry target.

In the corner of my eye, I glimpsed movement. A healthy, glowing canine ran down the hallway in slow motion like those gorgeous purebreds running through a field of daisies in dog food commercials. I was about to say, *Glenn, look at that gorgeous dog*, when I realized it was B.J.! How could that be?

This dog seemed young and happy and healthy, not the sad, sick dog we dropped off a few days before. Even her white muzzle seemed to disappear. My mind lagged seconds behind the reality that the light of my life had returned to me. Better than ever.

We crashed into each other, rolling over together across the linoleum floor. I didn't care that I looked ridiculous. I felt like a death-penalty felon who had been given the governor's reprieve.

I burrowed into B.J.'s feathery, golden coat in the back seat of Glenn's Toyota pick-up truck while Glenn steered us home, stoic and stalwart like the captain of the Titanic. We were hopeful and giddy like the passengers of that grand vessel before the unfortunate iceberg loomed large in our peripheral vision, realizing there was nothing we could do to stop our fate.

⌒

The school year ended. I resisted saying goodbye to my seventh graders because they would be starting the new year without me.

Proud of my eighth graders moving on to high school, I didn't have time to lament anything when I had B.J. back, happier than I had seen her before we left Laura's ranch. Everything revolved around her.

While Glenn worked, B.J. and I resumed short runs around town and escaped for a few day-trips to Lake Tahoe. The vets cautioned me against allowing her to swim in public lakes and pools, so we chased Frisbees and tennis balls into ankle-high water. B.J. didn't push her limits.

She seemed perfectly content to stay at the water's edge with me, drinking only the water I brought. Neither of us wanted to challenge the glorious fate of time.

Glenn showed up at our doorstep every evening after work. B.J. waited patiently at the door, wagging her feather-duster tail for the man who adored her mother. I'm convinced that part of her recovery had to do with the fact that I had someone meant for me; and, I'm convinced, B.J. sensed I wouldn't be alone without her.

Glenn's presence in our lives motivated the majority of her will to stay strong. I will go to my grave believing B.J. wanted assurance that she could hand me off to someone who loved me when she no longer could.

Glenn encouraged me to rethink the camping trip he had already planned for mid-June. The three of us needed to celebrate. I agreed. We cleaned out his parents' trailer and packed it with food, games, dog toys, bedding, and a suitcase full of excitement. The kite club had a weekend trip planned on the bluffs of Bodega Bay facing the Pacific Ocean. The perfect getaway.

It all came together because B.J. gifted me with her will to improve. With the school year over and Glenn in our lives, we started the summer with a pact to forget our worries. I needed time to stand still so that B.J. and I could wallow in the present, leaving the future as a distant star, light years away.

If I couldn't spend an eternity with her, at least we had the summer of 1994.

Ocean winds blew hard against the bluffs standing majestic above Highway 101. We camped outside the fishing town of Bodega Bay, north of San Francisco, where Alfred Hitchcock filmed his iconic movie, "The Birds." The kite club rented this space on top of the bluffs, the size of a few football fields, to accommodate dozens of trucks, sports vehicles, and trailers.

We parked in a wagon train circle to ward off the cutting chill of gale force winds that rattled our trailers, rocking incessantly throughout the long weekend. Tall grass and wild flowers grew in random patterns around the periphery of the land. The Pacific Ocean filled the horizon, serving as the perfect backdrop for the colorful kite displays looped on a constant stream from sunrise to sunset. When I closed my eyes, I became that eight-year-old girl at her backyard circus party.

Glenn woke up each morning at sunrise to walk B.J. in the flower fields. She sat at the trailer door next to her red leash the moment she heard Glenn get out of bed. I smiled with my eyes closed, grateful those two had formed a separate relationship.

One morning, I followed Glenn and B.J. past the campers and hid in the tall grass just to get a glimpse of my girl having fun without me. Glenn foraged through the brush like an intrepid hiker, B.J. followed dutifully behind. Glenn often turned back to B.J. with an encouraging word, probably sharing his interest in nature and making sure she was doing well.

I couldn't see her through the overgrown wild flowers; yet, her feathery red tail waved back and forth like a metronome, tick tock, tick tock, iridescent against the morning sun. I tiptoed back to the camper to make breakfast.

We flew several of Glenn's dual line kites in the afternoons. B.J. found a spot in the shade and watched our kites swoop and swirl around hundreds of other dancing kites. Many laughs and swear words escaped when a kite or two became tangled, crashing to the ground.

It was like watching the aftermath of bombed-out fighter planes plunging into the sea. No tempers flared if a kite string broke or a nylon panel tore. We hung suspended in the thrall of color, movement, laughter and camaraderie. B.J. and I savored those moments. Nights centered around a huge bonfire situated in the middle of the circular camper train. Musicians brought out guitars, flutes, and conga drums to accompany people brave enough to sing. Libations and laughter flowed. Happy sitting between Glenn and B.J., I reflected on the glow of the fire that sparkled in their eyes. I had it all.

Glenn moved in with us by mid-summer. He returned home to touch bases with his renter each day, but B.J. and I needed him more. By early August, I met with my new colleagues and moved into my new classroom. B.J. accompanied me while I unpacked stacks of boxes and designed my bulletin boards. Glenn and I focused so keenly on work, we didn't notice the imperceptible changes that had marked B.J.'s decline.

When her appetite waned and her luxurious coat lost its sheen, I refused to acknowledge the inevitable. I concentrated on B.J.'s passions—waiting by the door for Glenn and bringing us her leash for our nightly walk around town. I wouldn't admit to defeat.

Glenn competed in a kite club contest on a San Francisco beach in late August. I worried that B.J. couldn't last through the long day, but she rallied to the cause, eating her normal amount of prescribed kibble before we left. Glenn flew his stunt kite to Kenny Loggins' up-beat song, "Danger Zone." The ocean breezes blew hard.

B.J. and I sat in the sand wrapped in a blanket, my hair whipping around our faces. We watched Glenn's lean body running back and forth on the beach, directing his kite like a seasoned puppeteer. I shouted chants of encouragement while hugging B.J. into my chest.

My life with B.J. rewound to the rhythm of Glenn's kite—dipping, diving, and swirling around in my head. Carefully spliced and edited memories danced in my mind from the day Ben and I brought her home to the A-frame in Park City, through the divorce, my father's death, Dr. Laura's ranch, Chuck's Victorian house, and finding Glenn flying kites on the corner of Sunset Boulevard and Highway 65—all there in front of me. The wind scattered my tears in freeway patterns across my face as I meditated into the sun. When I looked down at B.J. snug in my lap, she was looking back up at me, smiling from floppy ear to floppy ear. My loyal, golden girl.

Glenn won first place! No one looked as gorgeous, nor moved as gracefully that day on the beach, harnessing the wind on the end of two nylon strings. A red Golden Retriever and a woman in love watched in awe.

B.J. turned eleven on August 28th, 1994. I celebrated my fortieth birthday in June. Glenn, four months shy of forty-four. I didn't know Boogers' exact age, but I estimated she recently turned fourteen. All of us, seasoned veterans in life.

I threw us a birthday party in the backyard. Glenn barbecued ribs in a pointy party hat I made him wear. We played barefoot in the grass with B.J's new toys.

I baked a cake, lemon with chocolate frosting. I decorated it with the candy words, "Mommy Loves You." We sang silly birthday songs. I watched from my mind's eye and recorded everything.

CHAPTER THIRTY

BOGEY

The 1994-95 school year at Phoenix High School began with a bang. Because of the enormous learning curve I had to navigate, finessing older teens with a more stringent curriculum, I kept B.J. at home. Her health frayed around the edges—dry dull coat, visible ribs, and cloudy eyes. The vets advised me to keep her exposure to a minimum.

Boogers continued caretaker duty, alerting me of B.J.'s status when I walked in the door. My trusty feline communicated her updates upon my arrival. If B.J. had a good day, Boogers didn't move from her spot on the bed, if B.J. had been in pain, Boogers met me at the door, pawing at my leg.

I had been thinking about another dog for B.J. because the memories of her days romping on the ranch with Tybo came back weighing heavy on my heart. B.J. liked a playmate when I worked. I grasped at straws to make B.J. feel better. Glenn and I could no longer be with her constantly as we had during those idyllic, kite-filled, summer days.

As if my guardian angel had read my thoughts, I received a call from a teacher friend whose cattle ranch wasn't far from Chuck's property in the outskirts of Lincoln.

"Hi Jeaninne, this is Bonnie. We've been fostering a stray dog on the ranch all week. I don't have the heart to place him in a shelter unless we can find him a good home. I was wondering if you and Glenn might know of anyone who could make room for this guy. He's a Border Collie and Labrador Retriever mix. I'm guessing he's around one or two, energetic but very sweet. We'd keep him, but we have too many dogs and cats as it is."

My heart quickened. *Could this guy be the one for our girl? He may be too young and energetic, but this has to be a sign.*

"Wow, you don't even know how timely this call is, Bonnie. As you know, B.J. is very sick. Maybe a new friend would cheer her up. I hate that she's in the yard alone when we are at work. Boogers is good to her, but a cat isn't the same.

Glenn and I will come by after work tomorrow. See you then."
I knew Glenn would approve. I ran into the den to tell him the
good news.

We drove in on the long dirt road between two fields of
horses and cows. A white wooden fence bordered the road on
either side. I saw Bonnie standing by the house holding on
to a large black dog with a white chest wiggling in her grasp.
We parked in the driveway, next to the kitchen door where
they stood. Bonnie let go of the dog. He charged at us with
the speed of Wile E. Coyote chasing the Road Runner in those
1960's Warner Bros. cartoons. I ducked behind Glenn before
he pounced on Glenn's chest, knocking us into the car. Glenn
laughed. I screamed. *This energetic dog will kill B.J.!*

"I don't know Bonnie, he may be too much for B.J." In my
mind's eye, I saw this wild canine running B.J. ragged in the
yard. He might kill her with love before I had to worry about
her kidneys taking her first.

Glenn, the practical optimist, said, "Let's walk around with
him and see what he does."

We walked through the horse fields with this beautiful boy
trailing behind, in front, on either side, and in circles around
us. His perpetual grin allowed his floppy tongue to sling saliva
everywhere. He exhausted me.

Bonnie hugged us. "Thanks for coming to see this exuberant young man. I understand he's too energetic for B.J. Let me know how she's doing." She looked sad, I felt bad.

As we drove down the road, dust flying everywhere, a black bullet sped up behind us. Glenn stopped the car. That goofy dog jumped up on Glenn's window and pawed at him. Glenn looked over at me with pleading, puppy-dog eyes. I said, "Okay, let him in."

We named him Bogey. As an avid golfer, Glenn came up with the term, which means one over par. Bogey was definitely one over par when it came to his unabashed spirit. He tried to be good, but he was young and enthusiastic, overjoyed to have found his forever home.

Amazingly, Bogey sensed B.J.'s illness from their first meeting in our house that evening. He sniffed her gently and gave her space. She looked at us with some confusion. I wondered if she thought, *Thanks, but no thanks. I don't have the stamina for this guy.* I wanted to give him back. *How could we have done this to her?*

Glenn and I discussed our resolve to make it work. Since we had already committed to arranging Bogey's puppy shots, a full check-up, and eventual neutering, we could have never given up on him. However, would B.J. ever approve? I felt like we had gone past the point of no return and it scared me.

That first night with Bogey, I escorted B.J. into our bedroom and shut the door.

"Oh, Sweetie, I know this is a huge change for you. We brought Bogey into our lives because he was homeless, scared, and lonely. I didn't want to upset you with all you are dealing with, but I couldn't help thinking of Tybo. You were there for him when he needed you. I thought maybe if Bogey had you, he wouldn't be so alone." My body shook with sadness.

B.J. licked my tear-stained face. "Listen to me, B.J. No one, I mean no one, could ever come between you and me. What we have is unbreakable—neither time, nor space, nor dimension can separate our love. And no matter what happens in the next few months, not even death can part us."

I almost vomited to expunge the pain in my soul.

I held her face between my hands, staring deeply into her eyes through the blurred vision of my tears, trying to steady my nerves.

"B.J., show me a sign that you are okay with this; if not, we will find Bogey a new home."

B.J. leaned into me, and then put her paw on my arm. I wanted to believe she was comforting me. *I'm so sorry, girl. About all of this.*

We didn't throw Bogey into B.J.'s personal space. We allowed them time together in the house under our supervision. I thought it prudent to keep B.J. in the house with Boogers when we were gone for a few hours, so that Bogey could run off his energy in the yard. When B.J. realized Bogey was going to stay, and that he only wanted to be her friend, we left them in the yard together.

Bogey watched B.J. like a hawk, never invading her personal space, except to give her a kiss every now and then. Boogers tolerated Bogey as if she understood we were bringing in new life for all of us.

Looking back, maybe Bogey was *my* distraction. Maybe, I needed a sparkly new toy to pull me out of my grief. We all knew the end was near for B.J., even this young, healthy pup with his life ahead of him seemed to sense that our time with her was limited and precious. Animals know.

Once our furry children adapted to Bogey's sweet presence, our home resumed its balance. I concentrated my love and attention on B.J. while Glenn spent time training and playing with Bogey.

B.J. continued to accompany me to the gym so she could watch our kite friends on the grassy knolls from her backseat window. And, she continued to be the official gym greeter, tied-up in the covered entryway where I could see her from my Stair Master, receiving pats and well wishes from patrons coming and going.

Glenn made sure B.J. knew that she would always be his favorite girl. He pulled her up on the couch with him every night for cuddle time in front of the fire. I took Bogey for long runs out of town where the ranch lands began. Boogers remained queen of the house.

CHAPTER THIRTY-ONE

Vows

The fall of 1994 arrived unannounced. Overnight, cold autumn breezes replaced the hot summer winds. A soft amber glow dimmed the days of the summer solstice's searing light. B.J.'s blood transfusion began to fade. We kept her home and comfortable, her walks became a thing of the past.

One evening in October, when our babies were curled on the rug in front of the fire, Glenn and I discussed our living situation.

"You know, Glenn, we're paying on two homes. What would be a good way to remedy one unnecessary mortgage/rent payment?"

I knew we would be together for the rest of our lives.

"Let's get married." Glenn doesn't mince words when it comes to practical matters. Even though we had only known each other since May, we had already shared a lifetime. I bounced off the couch and danced around the room, taking turns hugging B.J., Boogers and Bogey.

"Daddy and Mommy are going to be official, my lovelies!" I grabbed Glenn off the couch to join me in my dance around the room while our furry babies watched in wonder.

Glenn had clearly given it some thought. "We could move into my house and fix it up until we're ready to buy something else." I hadn't thought that far ahead and what it would mean for uprooting B.J., again. She and Boogers would miss the large Maple trees shading the pond of earthly delights. I would miss being close to work. Truth be told, I feared B.J. would give up with another move.

I hated the idea of leaving this stately Victorian for Glenn's 1970's tract home, but it made perfect sense. He owned, I rented. His house wasn't unique, but the large yard, perched high on a bluff, included a view that spanned the Sierra Mountain foothills to the east, the downtown buildings of Sacramento thirty miles to the west. I could work with that.

I made a quick calculation. "We don't need a big wedding. In fact, since your family will be in Southern California for Thanksgiving, why don't we get married in my mother's home that weekend? No one will have to make separate travel plans. If we limit it to immediate family, we can afford food, a cake, and champagne." Glenn liked that I had taken into account his family and didn't require anything expensive or fancy. We needed to save our money for renovating his house.

"Hi Mom. Are you seated?" I could barely contain my joy.

"Yes. I'm scared. Good news or bad?" Mom didn't like being surprised.

"Glenn and I set our wedding date for November 25th. We want to get married in your living room with just his family and mine. Is that okay?" I felt her approval before I heard the soft sniffles of joy.

"Really?! I'd be honored to host the wedding in our home. Wow, I need to get moving, don't I?" Mom loved to entertain. I almost heard her party planning wheels churning.

"I know, Mom. I'm jumping out of my skin with sheer bliss! I can't think of a better place to marry Glenn. Don't worry, we are paying for everything. We'll make it simple for you." I couldn't wait to help Mom with the details.

My mother met Glenn a month before this wedding conversation when I flew her up for her retirement present. Bowled over by his looks, his self-confidence, and his way around a kitchen, Glenn's stoic demeanor caught Mom off-guard. She realized how much Glenn loved me through his concern about my girls and Bogey. She was impressed by Glenn's respect for everything I valued. Mom called me after her weekend with us.

"Sweetie, what a good man. Glenn showed so much respect for you, B.J., Bogey, and Boogers. He was kind and solicitous with me. You deserve to be happy, my love."

Mom ordered the food, the cake, and the minister the next day. I called Julie to tell her that we would give her as much time as she needed to rent out her grandparents' Victorian. She assured us that we could stay until the following summer. Julie understood we had two households to join while working, not to mention navigating B.J.'s health. Glenn also needed time to ease out his renter. B.J. brought so many wonderful people into my life. A life that had become my destiny.

We collected our furry family in the living room to share the news. B.J. snuggled into my lap; Bogey leaned into Glenn; Boogers looked up nonchalantly before she changed positions on the couch.

I needed my babies to know that they would be cared for while we were away for our four-day wedding weekend. "Don't worry, my loves, Aunt Bonnie offered to care for you on her ranch as a thank you for adopting Bogey.

She assured me that Boogers and B.J. would have the run of the house. Bogey can run with the horses, but he will be in at night, tucked in with you girls." They probably didn't understand the gist of my conversation, but my voice and body language seemed to communicate that something was going to change for them soon. I needed to console myself that they would be protected in our absence.

My life rained blessings beyond belief in the fall of 1994.

Until it didn't.

My teaching position at the continuation high school fell into place like greeting an old friend. I enjoyed the challenge of older teens and the opportunities I made for writing new program grants. Glenn researched jobs within the California Department of Corrections because he grew weary of middle management. As with Ben, Glenn had dreams that needed to be fulfilled. He often wondered what it would be like to work in corrections. I supported this pursuit wholeheartedly.

Yet, the majority of our focus had to be on B.J.

One evening in early November, Glenn attended a special California Department of Corrections symposium, so I alternated the pup walks. Bogey beat me to the door to do our long run while B.J. waited patiently for her stroll through town. Bogey and I had just returned from our run feeling jovial and refreshed. However, B.J. wasn't at the door to greet us.

I found her curled up by the fireplace. "Come on, B.J., it's our turn to visit your favorite shopkeepers. They miss you if we don't walk by each evening."

B.J. couldn't get up.

I dove to her side on the living room rug. Lying head-to-head, I whispered, "Do you need to potty, Sweetie?"

That desperate throbbing in the pit of my stomach returned with a vengeance.

B.J. thumped her tail. Bogey slid down next to her, sniffing her face in between intermittent sweet licks. He knew.

"Give us some space, Mr. Bogey, I have to carry our girl outside to go potty. Such a good boy." I never imagined I would have to see this exuberant pup look so defeated. He loved B.J., too.

How could I have ever doubted accepting you into our home, Bogey boy?

B.J. struggled to get up, but her weak legs failed. I lifted her from under her hips until she could stand. Slowly we walked, my arms wrapped around her back end, until I had to carry her down the three steps to the side lot. I watched in horror while she tried to urinate what little fluid she had left, reminding me of the wobbly legs of a newborn filly. With my veil of denial lifted, I couldn't ignore how thin and frail she had become.

I died a little.

We managed to enter the house the way we exited. B.J. gave me every ounce of her love strength to pull her own weight. I arranged her futon bed on the floor in the living room, vowing to sleep with her that night. Bogey joined her on the futon while I made a call. A new respect for Bogey, my goofy guy, brought me to tears.

"Laura, it's Jeaninne." I inhaled deeply, holding my breath for a few seconds before exhaling, " B.J."

I choked on her name.

"I know, Jeaninne. I've been dreading this call."

Glenn didn't arrive home fast enough for me. He sensed how our moods had shifted. When he saw B.J. and Bogey on the futon, he knew we weren't having a slumber party. He slumped down next to us, caressing B.J.

Glenn didn't speak. He waited for me to tell him everything.

We sat with B.J. and Bogey on the futon mattress discussing our options for the difficult road ahead. Looking forlorn, Glenn mindlessly stroked B.J.'s back, over and over, just like he did when he met her seven months before.

I gently circled her silky ears through my nervous fingers. Bogey curled up at the end of the mattress, seemingly mindful of our space to get through this hard conversation. Anxiously twitching her tail, Boogers perched above us along the back of the couch. Loyal, dependable Boogers. Our rock.

"Laura told me that all we could do is assess her situation daily. As long as B.J. could still walk a bit, eat a little, and enjoy our company, we may have a week to ten more days, or less. She said we would know. Laura also instructed us to call her and she would alert her staff for our arrival. Oh Glenn, the wedding. You know I would cancel everything for B.J." My migraine headache alerted me that my body was on mental, physical, and emotional overload.

Glenn nodded. We turned out the lights and huddled around our girl until daybreak. The wedding was the last thing on our minds.

The nightmares that began when B.J. first lost her appetite varied. Sometimes, the despair woke me out of a deep sleep. Sometimes, dark places prevented me from finding her. Sometimes, I couldn't reach B.J. in time. She was tied up next to a white stucco building under a black iron stairwell, but my legs wouldn't move.

The week before our wedding, the dreams changed.

I limped through the final days with my students before the Thanksgiving break. I promised Glenn and my mother that I wouldn't change any wedding plans until the weekend we were scheduled to drive down, which gave us almost a week before our wedding day. I kept up my cheerful facade because my students expressed so much joy for our wedding. The staff and students gave me a wedding shower at work, so I owed them my gratitude.

My students also knew about B.J.'s terminal illness, but they refused to talk about it. Unlike my younger students, at-risk adolescents have experienced more heartache and loss; they were trying to spare my feelings.

They didn't know B.J. like my middle school students did, but they felt my pain.

The night before we were scheduled to drive to my mother's house, I tucked B.J., Bogey and Boogers in their beds beneath our four-poster bed, the one Ben built. I kissed Glenn goodnight and rolled over on my side. I thought about how we had arranged for B.J.'s care with Bonnie, my dear friend who had raised and mourned animals all of her life. Laura was also on call.

Bonnie promised me that she was capable of handling any scenario regarding B.J. I sobbed into my pillow feeling the depth of how much B.J. was loved by so many. Sleep came like a wave that crashed on the beach and swept me out to sea.

B.J. and I were hiking in Utah's Wasatch Mountain Range, the mountains of her youth. A giant orange moon hung over the treetops. We stopped on the edge of a cliff to count the moon's craters. Everything was bathed in moonlight. B.J. sat at attention next to me, her face tilted toward the light. She was calm, even peaceful. I couldn't move my body, but my hand stroked the back of her neck where her hair was thick and silky and warm. She looked up at me with such intense love, I couldn't contain it. My body floated above her.

It's time, Mommy.

I know, B.J., but I can't let you go.

You must let me go. I've waited too long.

What do you mean, Sweetie?

I promised to fight this pain until I knew you would be loved again. My mission is done. Be grateful, Mommy. My suffering can end.

In a flash, my body slammed to the ground. My girl flew over me with a comically long stick in her mouth, her favorite kind. I reached up to grab it, but she was gone.

"Glenn!" I sat up sobbing. "Glenn, wake up. We need to check on B.J. Now."

CHAPTER THIRTY-TWO

LOVE ETERNAL

Just before daybreak, Glenn accompanied Bogey out to the back yard to give B.J. and I our privacy. I joined B.J. under the bed. Her breathing, labored and shallow, she could no longer move. I held her close, thanking her for my life. I promised her that we would meet again. We levitated together. We levitated in a love we couldn't contain.

"Glenn, call Bonnie and Laura. We have to take her in today." Glenn understood the dream and had begun arranging her bed in his Chevy Blazer for our drive up to Mother Gold Vet Hospital. We decided to take Bogey and Boogers to Bonnie's ranch on our way up the hill, as well as postponing our drive down to my mom's for the following day.

We needed to be alone with B.J. We needed to say goodbye. It broke my heart to hear my mother's sobs on the other end of the line. I couldn't talk much, except to tell her that the wedding was still on as planned. B.J. would have wanted it that way. My mother always knew what to say. In that moment, it was no different.

"Glenn is B.J.'s gift to you. She has fulfilled her promise."

Bonnie met us at the car to retrieve our other two babies and to share her loving memories of B.J. I appreciated that kind gesture at a time when I sorely needed one. Bogey and Boogers kissed and nuzzled on their beloved friend.

B.J. thumped a weary tail for her pals, especially for Boogers, who had traveled this journey with her, every step of the way. I tried not to cry. I had to be strong until I couldn't be strong anymore. I had to save some strength for the ones she was leaving behind. I promised B.J. that I would.

With B.J.'s head in my lap, I focused on the dense pine trees lining Highway 49, the main road up to Grass Valley, north of Interstate 80. It was the road B.J. and I had traveled for eleven years—to and from my teaching jobs, to and from the first jobs Ben and I secured in Sacramento, to and from Chuck's ranch in Lincoln. It was the road that had connected our lives. It had to be the road that led her to her final rest.

318

I thought of the previous night's dream—the moon and the stars and the trees…and us. The perfect goodbye.

I stared at the back of Glenn's glossy black ponytail as he steered us to our fate. I stared at B.J.'s golden body, perfect in its shrunken form. I listened to her breathing. I kissed her face. I drank in her essence, not wanting to forget. Anything.

B.J. focused her cloudy gaze upon my tear-stained face. I felt what might be her words.

> *"Now that you will be marrying Glenn, I can go peacefully. I am so happy for you. Glenn is your true love. Thank you, Mommy, for giving me the best life a girl could ever have. I'm sorry about Papa Ben, but you both did your best for me, and for each other as long as you could. I will miss so many things—Glenn, Boogers, our runs, comforting your students, Lake Tahoe, the kites, Dr. Laura, Tybo, Chuck, Bogey, but mostly you. You want to know a secret, Mom? As much as I love you, I've always known that you've needed me more. Please love Glenn now with the same passion you've given to me since the first day you brought me into your life eleven years ago. This is my gift to you."*

We pulled into the parking lot. Time stopped.

Glenn busied about the car arranging B.J.'s blanket. I held on to her as if she were the last living being on the planet, keeping me safe in the middle of a dark, empty world.

Glenn rubbed my back. "I'll go check her in." For the last time, I buried my face into her soft, silky hair, smelling her essence, willing her to live. Selfishly, not wanting to let her go.

When he returned, he guided me gently out of the back seat in order to wrap our girl in the blanket we used for her futon bed to protect her thin frame from the cold. I walked beside Glenn, B.J. swaddled in his arms, while I stroked her head.

The office staff dabbed at their tears. My knees buckled with the realization of B.J's far-reaching love. Glenn supported me to the bench while we waited. I felt completely numb. I thanked the staff with my eyes. Everyone smiled, averting their gaze. They felt my pain.

Dr. Chris walked out to greet us. He explained that Laura couldn't make it from Carmel, but sent her love. I wanted her to be happy. She had already sacrificed so much for us. I also knew that it wouldn't have been right to have Laura administer this final act. I wanted B.J. to remember her in better times. Dr. Chris, the only one who could complete her destiny.

It felt preordained. And sacred.

The doctor outlined the procedure—the first shot a sedative, the second shot to stop the heart. I grabbed onto Glenn's arm. My knees buckled. I felt faint. "I can't do this. I can't go in. Please hold her, Glenn. Please do this for us. B.J. will understand. We have already said our goodbyes in my dreams."

Glenn nodded. B.J's eyes seemed to soften with relief. Dr. Chris squeezed my arm. The office staff turned away. I had to remember her alive.

I kissed B.J.'s nose, her eyes, and her mouth. I inhaled her remaining life force from the top of her head until I grew dizzy. I whispered, "Mommy loves you...always and forever."

I ran to the car. I cried for her. I cried for me. I cried for my students. I cried for Boogers and Bogey. I cried for Mom. I cried for anyone who had ever loved her. I even cried for Ben. However, I forgot to cry for Glenn.

B.J. and Glenn had conspired to leave him out of my grief. She wanted Glenn to take her place. She wanted him to remain that impenetrable force we both fell in love with; the only man who could have held it together for us these past six months. The only man who could have held her in his strong, loving arms. The only man.

Glenn arranged with the desk to have B.J. cremated. I wanted her ashes to be with us wherever our life led. We made a vow to include instructions in our trust that B.J.'s ashes would be mixed in with ours. Until death do us part.

Glenn returned to the car holding her red woven collar, the metal tags clinking together in a random lullaby. He placed it carefully in my hands. I clutched on to it, smelling her. I thought of the lock of hair I had snipped off of B.J. before we left the house that morning. I looked out the window to keep from falling apart. Glenn had been through enough.

When I turned to ask him about her final moments, I was taken aback by the tears streaming down his face. I realized I had never seen Glenn cry.

"Are you okay?" I patted Glenn's firm leg.

He wiped his nose with his sleeve. "I'm fine."

"Oh Glenn, I shouldn't have made you do that without me."

"No, she passed peacefully. It was beautiful."

"Really?" *Oh Jeaninne, why didn't you go in with him?*

"Yes. I…" Glenn tried to swallow the lump in his throat.

"What, honey?"

"I feel like I've lost my best friend."

CHAPTER THIRTY-THREE

A Legacy

B.J. died on November 20th, 1994. Glenn and I married on November 25th, 1994. B.J. had planned her exit perfectly. The wedding was short, simple and everything we wanted. Thirty close family and friends celebrated with us. I wore a long-sleeved, antique lace, cocktail dress with a sweetheart neckline. I also wore my mother-in-law's pearls and tucked my mother's blue trimmed lace handkerchief into my sleeve for something borrowed, something blue. I held a bouquet of long-stemmed white roses tied in a white silk bow. Glenn wore a black suit, white shirt and paisley tie. I let my long curly hair flow naturally. Glenn pulled his hair back at the nape of his neck. We honored B.J. in our vows.

Glenn's family brought trays of fresh sushi and delectable Japanese desserts. My mother provided chicken casseroles, a variety of salads, dinner rolls, dry champagne and the two-tiered wedding cake. We married in her lovely living room to the background music of Barbra Streisand's "Evergreen."

We ate and celebrated in my parents' festive kitchen/family room, a fire roaring in the fireplace. We spent two nights in Rosarita Beach, Mexico, for our honeymoon. When we flew kites on the beach in remembrance of B.J., I felt her soaring above us, finally free of her pain and suffering.

The day of B.J.'s passing, we returned home from the Mother Gold Veterinary Hospital devastated and exhausted, yet thankful for all the things we needed to do for the wedding to keep us busy. Bonnie reported that Bogey and Boogers were doing just fine, and then she made me promise I would savor family and enjoy the wedding, exactly what B.J. would have wanted. The only time Glenn and I spoke that day was to share our favorite golden girl memories. We laughed, we cried, we remembered. Glenn folded up the futon bed because I couldn't look at the mattress that had supported her on all those painful nights. He put away her collar, her leash, her bowls and her toys for safe-keeping.

It would be months before I could look at them again. I urged Glenn to leave B.J.'s bed under ours. Bogey and Boogers eventually snuggled in it, keeping her essence close.

The night of her passing, after I turned out the lights, I whispered in Glenn's ear, "I hope B.J. speaks to me in my dreams. I need to know that she's alright." Glenn hugged me tightly.

I stood on our same cliff in the Wasatch Range. The starless night rendered me blind to everything but the vibrant contours of the giant moon. I heard the wind blowing through the trees. I wasn't cold, nor was I afraid. I counted the craters close enough to touch.

She was silhouetted against the soft lunar light, a black speck in the distance. As B.J. flew closer, I could see the joy in her eyes. She carried a large stick, reminding me of a tightrope walker's balance pole, teetering back and forth in the grip of her jaws. I jumped up to grab it, willing B.J. to take me with her. She dropped the stick into my hands.

It's yours now, Mommy. Guard it until we meet again.

I waved farewell, watching B.J.'s shiny golden coat disappear into the orange glow of the moon.

EPILOGUE

We renovated Glenn's Rocklin home throughout the winter and spring of 1995. Bogey and Boogers adapted well to the new house, but a deep part of me missed the Lincoln Victorian. It would always be the last home B.J. and I shared.

I immersed myself in my teaching, as well as writing grants for leadership scholarships and establishing a partnership between the high school and a Sacramento homeless shelter. Glenn worked as a counselor for at-risk teens until he was accepted into the academy to become a correctional officer for the California Department of Corrections. We lived our love, eternally grateful B.J. had brought us together.

A year to the day of B.J.'s passing, November 20, 1995, I woke up feeling blue. I waited to see if Glenn had remembered, but he said nothing to me that morning. I taught my classes with half a heart. I wanted to go home, dive under the covers, and forget that painful anniversary. Too distracted to go for my usual run after work, I apologized to Bogey and promised him a longer run the next day. I cuddled with Bogey and Boogers on the family room couch. We watched mindless old TV shows and waited for Glenn. Almost an hour after Glenn normally came home from CDC training, I vacillated between worry and anger.

> *God, please let Glenn be okay, and if he is, then he will get an ear full when he walks in the door. How could he forget our girl's passing? If it weren't for B.J., we wouldn't be living our destiny. I just want this day to end.*

When the front door opened, my anger turned from simmer to boil.

Glenn, who normally kissed me before settling in, yelled out a hello, and then ducked down the hall. *That's weird, what's up with him?*

I jumped up, Bogey at my heels, when I heard, "Jeaninne, I'm in the den."

I stomped into the den ready to battle, but stopped dead in my tracks when I saw the look on Glenn's face. Something about him was softer, more vulnerable.

He put both of his large warm hands on my shoulders and turned my body to face the Ikea cedar shelf against the wall.

"Do you see it?" I felt static electricity coming off his body.

A few seconds passed before my eyes focused on a small pine box adorned with a black and gold engraved plaque.

I looked up at the man I love.

"Read the plaque!" Glenn twitched with anticipation as he hugged Bogey into his legs.

I bent down and read:

B.J.

August 28, 1983 – November 20, 1994

"Mommy Loves You"